Excel
for Beginners

"No Experience Required!"

Updated
for
Excel 5

Abacus
A Data Becker Book

Rainer Bartel

Copyright © 1994, 1993   Abacus
5370 52nd Street SE
Grand Rapids, MI 49512

Copyright © 1993   Data Becker, GmbH
Merowingerstrasse 30
4000 Duesseldorf, Germany

Managing Editor:	Scott Slaughter
Editors:	Amy Venlos, Gene Traas
Technical Editor:	Gene Traas, George Miller
Book Design:	Scott Slaughter
Proofreader:	Robbin Markley
Cover Art:	Abby Grinnell

Printed in the U.S.A.

ISBN 1-55755-199-5

10 9 8 7 6 5 4 3 2

Excel For Beginners

Contents

v

Contents

14 Excel Terms You Should Know 185

Appendix A: Excel Sheets 189

Appendix B: Banania 213

Contents

Chapter 1

What Are All These Keys?

Do you know anyone who can launch into really technical discussions about computers without a lot of, or any, prodding? After listening to them for just a few minutes, you realize you're just nodding and smiling dumbly. You have no idea what they're talking about. Now here you are, trying to learn a computer application.

Excel doesn't require you to know a lot about computers. But there are a few things worth knowing. The best place to start is with the computer's hardware, all the physical (hard) components of your computer system.

Unlike your computer's "software" (programs that run on the computer), you can actually see and touch the computer hardware.

You use the keyboard and mouse to "talk with" the computer, giving it commands, responding to its cues, and entering information. You use the computer monitor to see what you're doing and to read the computer's responses and messages.

The Keyboard

The following illustration shows today's most common IBM-compatible keyboard, the "MF2" keyboard:

1 | What Are All These Keys?

MF2 keyboard

To explain your keyboard, we've divided it into different segments. Don't bother to memorize all this information. We'll refer to these keys and functions as they come up.

Key	Appearance	Key	Appearance
Alt	ALT, Alt, Alternate	Backspace	Backspace
End	END, End	Tab	TAB
Home	HOME, Home	PgUp	PageUp, PgUp
Ctrl	CTRL, Ctrl, Control	PgDn	PageDown, PgDn
Del	DEL, Del, DELETE, Delete	CapsLock	CAPS, Caps Lock, CAPS LOCK
Ins	INS, Insert	ScrollLock	SCROLL LOCK, Scroll Lock
Enter	Enter, Return	NumLock	NUM LOCK, Num Lock
ESC	ESCAPE, Esc, Escape	PrtSc	Print Screen, PRTSC, PrtSc
Shift	SHIFT		

The typewriter keys

Typewriter keys

If you ever used a typewriter, you should be familiar with most of these keys. This part of the computer keyboard even looks like a typewriter keyboard. Some of the keys have slightly different functions than their typewriter counterparts. The carriage return key (known as the Enter key in computer lingo), for instance, does more than just insert carriage returns, and Tab can be used for more than just making indentations.

Unlike nonelectric typewriters, most of the typewriter keys on your computer keyboard repeat. If you press m, for example, the letter "m" appears on your screen. If you hold m down a little bit, you'll see "mmmmmmmmmmm" across the screen.

Also, look for two exotic keys, Ctrl and Alt. These perform special functions within computer programs when they are combined with other keys.

The Enter key

For example, you can end a line and simultaneously start a new one just by pressing Enter in a word processing application. In Excel, it tells the application which numbers and texts you want in a table. You enter the numbers and texts through your keyboard, then confirm the entries by pressing Enter.

What Are All These Keys?

The Shift or Caps Lock key

You can enter uppercase letters on your computer keyboard the same way you do on a typewriter. If you hold one of the two Shift keys while pressing a letter key, that letter is typed uppercase. With the number keys above the letter keys, you hold the Shift key and press the number key to type the corresponding symbol.

If you want to enter only uppercase letters, you can use the Caps Lock key. Your keyboard might have a light that goes on when the Caps Lock key is activated. Return to the normal lowercase mode by simply pressing one of the Shift keys; some keyboards require you to press Caps Lock again.

Say you activate your Caps Lock key, then hold the Shift key down while you enter a letter. The Caps Lock and Shift keys cancel each other out, and the letter is displayed in lowercase.

TAKE NOTE

> The Caps Lock key has no effect on the number keys located in the typewriter keys. Even when Caps Lock is active, you still have to press Shift to type a symbol that's on a number key.

The Ctrl and Alt keys

The Ctrl and Alt keys (short for "control" and "alternate") are sort of like Shift. These keys have to be used in combination with another key to do anything. For instance, when you combine one of them with a function key (one of the "F" keys at the top of the keyboard), you send a command to the computer based on the program you're in. In Excel, you can perform many tasks very quickly when you use these key combinations.

TAKE NOTE

> You have to hold the Ctrl or Alt key down when you combine it with another key. While you're holding it down, press the combination key, then release both keys.

The Esc key

The Esc key (short for "escape") allows you to "escape" from many different situations. When you're in Excel, this key lets you abort various operations you started. For instance, you can use Esc to cancel the most recent text or number entry in a table.

The Backspace key

Everyone makes typing mistakes. Since you can't use correction fluid on your screen, you need another way to correct these mistakes. One way is to use the Backspace key, which operates the same way as on an electronic typewriter.

The function keys

The function keys do different things, depending on the program you're in. In Excel, the function keys do things that speed up your work. F1, for instance, is the key you press when you need help.

Excel offers additional shortcuts to your work by combining these keys with Ctrl and Alt. To execute one function, you might even use a complex combination like ⇧Shift + Ctrl + F3.

The cursor keys

The cursor keys allow you to quickly move the cursor or pointer around the screen. The cursor is a vertical blinking bar on your screen, indicating where you can enter text or numbers. To insert a character among other characters, just move the cursor to that position and type the desired character.

The four arrow keys allow you to move your cursor in any direction. The Home and End keys usually let you jump to the beginning or end of a line of text. The Pg Up and Pg Dn keys let you move from one screen page to the previous or next one, respectively. The End key also has special properties in an Excel table, which we'll discuss later.

Ins and Del are used for editing. Ins toggles between insert and overwrite modes of text entry. Del is used to erase selected text or the character immediately to the right of the cursor.

The numeric keypad

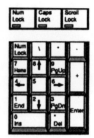

The numeric keypad's keys have double functions. For example, 4 can also be used as a left arrow key. The Num Lock key lets you switch between each key's functions. When it's activated, the Num Lock light on your keyboard should be lit.

In Excel, you'll probably want to leave the Num Lock function on. The keys are laid out like a calculator to make it more convenient for you to enter sequences of numbers. Remember to confirm all of your entries with Enter.

When the keyboard beeps

We discussed key repetition when we explained the typewriter keys: If you hold a key down, its character is repeated on your screen. If you hold down certain other keys, the computer beeps at you. The computer might also beep at you when you're simply trying to enter numbers or text, because you're typing faster than the computer can process your entries.

NERD TALK

If the computer is doing something else while you're typing, it can store a little of the stuff you're typing in a buffer. If this buffer fills up and you continue to type, the computer protests by beeping. Pause until the beeping stops, then continue to enter your information.

The Mouse

If your idea of working at the computer consists of entering long strings of commands on some bare-bones display screen, you'll be surprised at Excel. This application uses a piece of software called Windows, which fills your screen with pictures that tell you what the computer is doing, and what applications and commands are available. This is known as a graphical user interface.

Almost all technical devices have a user interface, even a car. Your car communicates to you through the speedometer, odometer, temperature gauge, fuel gauge, and other instruments; you talk to your car using the pedals, levers, and steering wheel. You communicate with your computer through the keyboard or a mouse, and Windows operates best with the mouse. Since Excel only functions when Windows is running on your computer, it also uses the mouse.

WARNING!

> You can only use Excel effectively if your PC is equipped with a mouse. Therefore, if you don't have a mouse as part of your computer system, you should install one before you begin working with Excel.

Different kinds of mice

There are mice with two buttons and with three. In your work with Excel, you'll want a mouse with at least two buttons. If you have a three-button mouse, you'll only use the left and right buttons; the center button won't serve any function under Excel.

Handle your mouse with care

As you know, all computer hardware, including your mouse, is fragile. Just as you do with every other piece of computer hardware, you should treat your computer mouse carefully.

1 | What Are All These Keys?

Be sure you're in Windows or Excel so you can see what the mouse movement looks like. Move the mouse across the desk or table and watch the pointer move across your screen. The mouse pointer lets you perform tasks on the screen. The best part is that you don't have to type extensive commands to operate the computer.

Clicking

The most simple operation you can do with your mouse is to click it. It's just like pushing a button. Move your mouse until the mouse pointer is on an icon (pick any symbol you want for this experiment). Once it's positioned on this icon, press the left mouse button briefly and release it immediately. Now you're clicking.

Usually you click the mouse to enter a command. In Excel, you select a table cell by putting the mouse pointer in this cell and clicking the left mouse button.

Often you'll see grey, 3D-looking, labeled rectangles on your screen. These are called buttons, and simulate the buttons you would find on a physical object, like a calculator. As you may have guessed, you click one of these buttons to trigger whatever action the label indicates.

The gray labeled rectangles are buttons you activate with mouse clicks.

Double-clicking

Double-clicking is a little trickier. Move the mouse pointer onto an icon and click the mouse button twice quickly. After you've done this successfully, the icon usually disappears and the screen transforms into a rectangular, bordered area called a window. If you didn't do this correctly, more than likely nothing will happen.

It may take a little practice to successfully double-click, because you have to do the motion just right. If you ever learned to drive a standard transmission car after driving an automatic one for so long, you might appreciate the practice needed for something like this. Eventually it'll become second nature.

Dragging

Think of the mouse pointer as an extension of your hand. Dragging is like putting your hand into the computer, then grabbing and moving things on the screen.

You'll probably want to experiment with dragging. Move the mouse pointer onto a movable icon or object, then press the left mouse button and hold it down. Now when you move the mouse, the object sticks with your mouse pointer. When you release the mouse button, the object stays where you released it.

How not to use the mouse

Perhaps you noticed that you can't move the mouse pointer while you're holding the mouse up in the air, regardless of how wildly you flail it. This is because the mouse's mechanical anatomy requires it to roll along a flat surface. Turn your mouse over and notice the roller ball in the hole on the underside. The movements of this ball are copied by the screen's mouse pointer. The ball can only move when the mouse rolls along on a flat surface.

We strongly suggest that you purchase what's called a mouse pad to roll your mouse on. It's usually rubberized, so it's comfortable for your wrist as well. You can get one at a computer supply store, an office supply store, or other places.

WARNING!

The roller ball needs to be kept clean. Be careful where you use the mouse. Don't roll it on any body parts, including your finger, and don't roll it on anything with a surface that might damage the mouse.

Chapter 2

Introducing Excel

Excel is a spreadsheet application. A spreadsheet is a program designed to calculate rows and columns of numbers based on the formulas you enter. Spreadsheets allow you to display and arrange information in a matrix of vertical columns and horizontal rows called worksheets. Your checkbook register is a perfect example of a worksheet.

The ability to arrange information this way makes Excel very useful. Consider how often you need to make lists. Even your grocery shopping would be more efficient if you arranged what you needed and their costs in a worksheet.

Excel lets you not only create worksheets, but also rearrange and move information in these worksheets. It offers many techniques you can use to construct and organize worksheets. When you print your work, you can use different fonts and font sizes, even different colors if you have the right hardware.

Worksheets

Once you start to look for them, you'll see worksheets everywhere. A restaurant menu is one example: Foods make up one column, and their respective prices make up another, with each pair comprising a row. A plane schedule is another example: destinations are listed in one column, and their respective departure times are listed in another, each set again making up a row.

The following illustrates a classic example of a worksheet, the mileage chart you find in most road atlases:

Introducing Excel

Road Mileage Between Selected U.S. Cities	Atlanta	Boston	Chicago	Cincinnati	Cleveland	Dallas	Denver	Des Moines
Atlanta, Ga.	0	1,037	674	440	672	795	1,398	870
Boston, Ms.	1,037	0	963	840	628	1,748	1,949	1,280
Chicago, Il.	674	963	0	287	335	917	996	327
Cleveland, Oh.	440	840	287	0	244	920	1,164	571
Cincinati, Oh.	672	628	335	244	0	1,153	1,321	652
Dallas, Tx.	795	1,748	917	920	1,153	0	781	684
Denver, Co.	1,398	1,949	996	1,164	1,321	781	0	669
Detroit, Mi.	699	695	266	259	170	1,143	1,253	584
Houston, Tx.	789	1,804	1,067	1,023	1,273	243	1,019	905
Indianapolis, In.	493	906	181	106	294	865	1,058	465
Kansas City, Mo.	798	1,391	499	591	779	489	600	195
Los Angeles, Ca.	2,182	2,979	2,054	2,179	2,367	1,387	1,059	1,727
Memphis, Tn.	371	1,296	530	468	712	452	1,040	589
Milwaukee, Wi.	761	1,050	87	374	422	991	1,029	361
Minneapolis, Mn.	1,068	1,368	405	632	740	936	841	252
New Orleans, La.	479	1,507	912	786	1,030	436	1,273	978
New York, N.Y.	841	206	802	647	473	1,552	1,771	1,119
Omaha, Ne.	986	1,412	459	680	784	644	537	132
Philadelphia, Pa.	741	296	738	567	413	1,452	1,631	1,051
Pittsburgh, Pa.	687	561	452	287	129	1,204	1,411	763
Portland, Or.	2,601	3,046	2,083	2,333	2,418	2,009	1,238	1,766
St. Louis, Mo.	541	1,141	289	340	529	630	857	333
San Francisco, Ca.	2,496	3,095	2,142	2,362	2,467	1,753	1,235	1,815
Seattle, Wa.	2,618	2,976	2,013	2,300	2,348	2,078	1,307	1,743
Tulsa, Ok.	772	1,537	683	736	925	257	681	443
Washington D.C.	608	429	611	481	346	1,319	1,616	384

Mileage chart from a road atlas

You can create a similar mileage chart by using Excel.

Calculations

Excel lets you perform calculations on the numbers you enter into the worksheets you create. You can use Excel simply to replace your pocket calculator, entering numbers you want to add, subtract, multiply or divide, then letting Excel calculate the result. After you've entered the numbers and told it how to calculate them, you can change one of the numbers and Excel will automatically recalculate.

However, Excel does more than just simple arithmetic. On a considerably higher level, Excel offers many possibilities for evaluating large amounts of data. This application can automatically determine the median, minimum, or maximum value in a series of numbers. It can also calculate complex financial or mathematical values, like the annual depreciation on your computer.

Other Neat Things Excel Can Do

Excel's main purpose is to create, organize, and evaluate worksheets mathematically. The majority of its commands and functions are geared toward these tasks. Among its other talents, Excel can let you create charts and manage data within its worksheets.

Charts

Sometimes, you might want to represent your worksheet information as a chart. The following is an example of a voting chart:

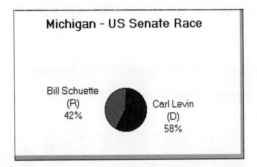

A voting chart makes the election more understandable

You can create remarkably attractive charts in Excel, using series of numbers and labels. Your own artistic touches refine charts visually to suit your needs, whether for a display of household chores or a sales presentation.

Databases

Imagine you want to make a directory of everyone in your bowling league. You can create a worksheet and put each member's last name in the first column. In the second column, you put their first names, in the third, their addresses and, in the fourth, their phone numbers. You don't need to enter the names alphabetically, because Excel can arrange them that way for you.

2 | Introducing Excel

Excel makes it easy to create and arrange lists. It effectively replaces your card file. Computer nerds call this a "database", which means a set of related information.

Using a handwritten card file to list the bowling league members means you have to sort the cards by hand. When you have to look for someone living in a particular area of town, you have to search card by card. Excel can sort not only by last or first name, but also by address. You decide how it arranges each of the electronic "cards".

Now imagine organizing all your videocassettes, CDs, recipes, or books in Excel worksheets. If you're into this sort of thing, this can be pretty exciting. And, with Excel, you can easily look up pieces of these lists, like all your videos that were produced in 1982, if that's part of the data you entered.

Excel's Limitations

Excel creates worksheets, calculates numbers in worksheets, creates charts from the data in worksheets, and manages data. Excel won't write letters to your in-laws for you. It won't compile all your class notes and write a term paper.

With Excel, you can't enter the minutes of last year's board meetings to create a report on the company. Excel doesn't have any programs for letting you draw pictures. And, if your goal is simply to play with your computer, Excel may be disappointing.

Chapter 3

Before Starting Excel

Although switching on a computer may sound easy, sometimes simply finding the switch can be frustrating because manufacturers place the switch in different locations. It can be in the front, side, or back of your CPU (the big rectangular part of your computer system, usually located under your monitor screen). Also, its color can be different, ranging from black, white, red, orange, or another color. It's usually a toggle switch that's labeled "On/Off" or "1/0". After you switch on the computer, it makes a single beep or other subtle sound.

Wait a few moments for the computer to begin displaying data on your monitor screen. If you don't see anything, you may have to switch on the monitor separately from the computer. The shape and location of the monitor on/off switch also vary. When the monitor is on, a small light (called the "idiot light") on the front of the monitor goes on.

Your computer may have many different lights and switches. One light may indicate whether the computer's main power is activated. Other computers have a light labeled "turbo". Some computers even have lights that indicate how fast the PC is operating. You can ignore these lights and switches for now.

Restarting the computer

You should pay attention to one button - the Reset button. It's probably on the front of the CPU. You may need it in some extreme situations.

WARNING!

Only use the Reset button in an absolute emergency.

The Reset button restarts the computer if it becomes "locked up" or when your keyboard or mouse pointer do not operate. This can happen even in Excel, and is called a computer "crash". If this happens to you, first try to return to Windows.

If you can't return to the Windows application, don't automatically use the Reset button. Press the Ctrl + Alt + Del buttons by holding down the first two of these keys with your left hand, pressing Del briefly with your right hand, then releasing all three keys. Your display monitor should change. If it doesn't respond, you need to press the Reset button.

Opening Windows

When the computer and monitor are on, the screen should show one of the following:

1. Technical data about your computer system may scroll down the screen, ending with "C:\>".

2. A colorful display covers the screen to indicate you're in Windows. This is the screen that you want to appear.

"C:\>" is what you see

The "C:\>" character is called the DOS prompt. It's also called the "ready prompt". It looks something like the following:

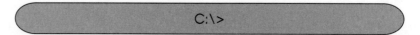

C:\>

From here, it's easy to start the Windows application and, from there, Excel. Enter the following text to start the program:

```
WIN Enter
```

Press Enter after typing "WIN" to tell the computer this is the command you want to execute.

Something other than "C:\>" is on your screen

The DOS prompt may not look exactly like "C:\>". It could be a variation, like C>, C:>, or even D:\>. And, of course, these aren't the only DOS prompts you might encounter. Other possible combinations could include the following:

- Letters from C through Z

- Letters with a colon

- Letters with a slash

- Letters with a greater than sign (>)

- Letters with a less than sign (<)

- Other punctuation marks can occur

The most important thing to look for is the blinking cursor to the right of the DOS prompt.

If something completely different appears on the screen, such as the following:

"(A)bort", "(R)etry", "(F)ail"

the computer is saying it can't find DOS - perhaps because it tried to read the diskettes in your drives first. You need to remove any diskettes from the disk drives and restart your computer using the Ctrl + Alt + Del key combination.

When you finally reach the DOS prompt, start the Windows interface. Windows should look something like this:

Before Starting Excel

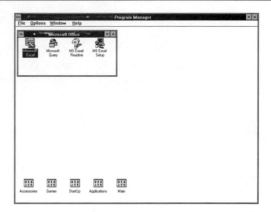

Windows after startup

You can't find Windows

If you get an error message instead of Windows when you try to call the program, Windows is either not installed or installed incorrectly on your PC. So, you'll need to install Windows; don't be afraid to ask for assistance or refer to the installation information later in this chapter.

Windows and Excel both include program diskettes and instructions for installing the software. Follow these instructions and the installation shouldn't be difficult.

Do-It-Yourself Program Installation

Usually, you can only start applications stored on your computer's hard drive. This includes applications like Windows and Excel. If you get an error message when you try to start Windows, something is wrong with your Windows application. You may have to reinstall the Windows interface on your PC.

QUICK TIP

Make certain you know what programs are stored on your hard drive, whether on your home computer or the one at work. If you don't know how to read the hard drive's directory, find someone that can help you get the information.

Installing Windows

If you feel confident to reinstall Windows yourself, we should forewarn you: There's no way to know what will be lost or retained during this new installation. Nevertheless, we recommend reinstalling Windows if nothing else seems to help. The following instructions are general installation steps:

1. Use the original Windows diskettes.

2. Remove any diskettes still in the disk drives. Perform a warm boot by pressing the Ctrl + Alt + Del key combination or press the Reset button. The computer should eventually display the DOS prompt, followed by a blinking cursor. If you don't get this prompt after the warm boot, there's probably something wrong with your computer that only an expert can handle.

3. Place the first Windows diskette in your drive. (Usually we recommend that you copy these original diskettes and use the copies for the installation to avoid accidentally damaging the originals.)

4. Enter the letter of the drive. Remember to enter the colon after the drive letter. Then press Enter.

TAKE NOTE

Always press Enter after typing a command on the DOS command line. Otherwise, DOS won't know that the command should be executed.

5. Enter the command that will start the Windows installation:

SETUP Enter

If you get an error message after you enter this command, you probably inserted the wrong diskette. Make certain you inserted the first diskette.

6. The Setup program will display different instructions. Follow these until you complete the procedure.

When you're done, your Windows interface should function properly. If it still doesn't work right, repeat these steps or contact someone familiar with your system. Your computer's basic settings may be incorrect and only someone who is familiar with your PC can help.

Installing Excel

You'll have to install Excel if it isn't on your hard drive. If you have the original Excel diskettes, it should be easy to do. However, first you'll need to be in Windows (see prior section):

1. Place the first Excel diskette in the appropriate disk drive and start Windows. Type:

    WIN [Enter]

2. Open the **File** menu in the Windows Program Manager, and select **Run....**

3. Look for a small window containing a text box. Enter the source drive, then the command SETUP. The source drive, usually Drive A:, contains your floppy diskette.

4. Click [OK] and you'll start the installation program with the first Excel diskette.

As in Windows, the program gives you various instruction screens so you know what's going on and what to do next. Simply follow these instructions.

When the installation is done, you'll automatically go back to the Program Manager. Now you should see a group icon for Excel here.

Accessing Excel

After starting the Windows interface, a window will appear on your screen. That's how Windows got its name. The screen displays everything in windows, which always have a border and a title bar at the top telling you what's running in that window.

The Program Manager always appears first when you start Windows. It shows what applications are available and lets you select one.

Why the Program Manager shrank

From a window covering the whole screen, the Program Manager can reduce itself to a little picture with its name on it in one part of the screen. This picture is called an icon. There might be other icons on the screen, depending on how Windows was installed, but you can ignore these for now.

If the Program Manager is only an icon, double-click it to open the window. You need to be in this window to get to Excel. If you don't double-click correctly, you get a box called the Control menu, which lists all possible commands line by line.

You can double-click the icon until the Program Manager is finally opened or you can simply click the Program Manager icon once, then select **Maximize** from the menu options. At this point, the Program Manager window should finally open.

If your Program Manager looks different

If someone else has used your Windows interface after you worked on it, the Program Manager window's appearance may have changed. It's possible to change a window's appearance and, when you exit Windows, these changes are also saved. Unless someone else uses your computer system, your interface will look exactly the way you left it when you start it up the next time.

Before Starting Excel

Icon groups

The Program Manager contains several group icons. They should be arranged in a row along the bottom of the window. If they aren't, you can rearrange them. Click the Window menu in the Program Manager's title bar, and drag your mouse pointer to the Arrange icons option. Release the mouse button, and your option should briefly flicker on the screen. After that, the icons in your window should now look tidy.

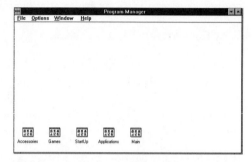

Program Manager window and the standard icons

Although your Windows screen may appear different, the Program Manager should contain at least the following five icons: "Accessories", "Games", "Start Up", "Applications", and "Main".

Look for Excel's icon group

What you're really looking for among all these icons is one called Excel. Don't panic if you cannot find it immediately because it may appear under a different name, such as:

    "Excel"   "MS Excel"

    "Microsoft Excel"   "Microsoft Office"

    "Excel Group"

Starting Excel

However, if you can't find any Excel icon, simply look in the corresponding group window. When you find it, the icon for Microsoft Excel Version 5 looks like the icon to the right:

If you open a window and don't find what you're looking for, exit that window. Find a special button for the Control menu at the left end of the title bar. It looks like a small square with a dash. Double-click this button to close the window.

Practice opening and closing windows: Double-click each icon, then close it again by double-clicking the Control menu. This is illustrated in the figure to the right:

Once you've found the Excel icon (or other corresponding name) in either the Excel group or in the "Applications" group, you're ready to start Excel. Double-click the Excel icon. This application takes a moment to start so the computer will display a small hourglass.

This lets you know it'll be a little while before the application is ready. Then it displays a rectangle with Excel's name on it. Finally, your screen becomes the Excel window. This is your confirmation that the program started successfully.

When You're Finally in Excel

Excel starts out displaying a default workbook in its application window. You'll remember we discussed worksheets earlier in this book - a workbook is a collection of worksheets (more on this later).

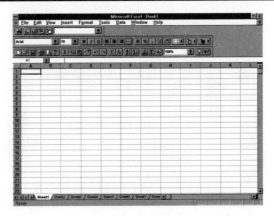

Excel upon startup

The workbook window's name is displayed in the title bar at the top of the window. The workbook window contains a blank worksheet when Excel starts. This sheet is called "Sheet1", as shown by the tab at the bottom of the sheet.

When Excel starts, the Excel application-default window combination usually fills the screen and obscures any other open windows. However, Excel lets you know that other windows are open. A special button at the right end of the title bar contains two triangles, one pointing up and one pointing down.

> You might not see the Excel window on the screen if Excel is an icon at startup. Simply double-click the Excel icon and it'll take you into the window.

TAKE NOTE

It's also possible that your Excel window won't cover the entire screen, but will appear as a smaller window on your screen. This only happens if someone else used Excel on your PC and changed some settings. Click the triangle pointing up to increase the size of the window. This is called "maximizing" the window.

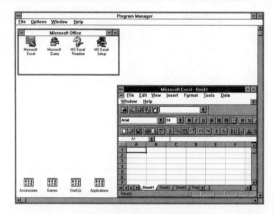

Excel as a smaller window

If the window is suddenly an icon, you probably clicked the triangle pointing down by accident. Double-click the icon and you'll return to the window. Then click the triangle pointing up to enlarge the window.

Viewing the Excel windows

The Excel application window has all the basic elements found in other application windows:

Remember, by double-clicking the Control-menu box (the button with the dash), you can close a window.

Below the title bar is the menu bar containing the individual menu names. Click the name of the menu you want to open, then select one of the menu items.

Like most other applications that run under Windows, Excel has the **File**, **Edit**, and **Help** menus in its menu bar.

QUICK TIP

Don't be surprised if the menu names differ and menus aren't always available. Excel transforms the menu bar to adjust to different situations when some things can or can't be done.

Below the menu bar is the toolbar. It contains several buttons and at least one display box. You can consider the toolbar as Excel's control panel. Each button refers to a command or series of commands. Click one of these buttons to trigger the corresponding command. This can really speed up your productivity. We'll discuss this in more detail later.

The workbook window is a blank Excel worksheet with numbers for the rows and letters for the columns. Look for scroll bars in this window that let you scroll up and down as well as across the worksheet.

NERD TALK

> The Excel application window can contain several workbook windows simultaneously. To make all this manageable, each workbook window includes Minimize and Maximize buttons so you can turn any worksheet window into an icon and make room for other workbooks. We recommend that you maximize the workbook window you're using by clicking the triangle pointing up in the title bar of that workbook window.

When the workbook window is Maximized, it doesn't have a title bar. The title of the workbook is displayed next to the application title. The Maximize and Minimize buttons for the workbook are displayed at the right side of the menu bar.

Problems Starting Excel

Several different problems can occur when you start Excel. The following are a few possible solutions:

When you switch your computer on, you don't see the Windows interface

Enter WIN in the DOS command line where you see the blinking cursor and press Enter.

The Windows interface doesn't appear even after entering the WIN command

This means your PC's basic settings are incorrect or Windows isn't installed on your computer.

Try entering CD WINDOWS on the command line with the blinking cursor, then pressing [Enter] to confirm. If you don't get any error messages, like "Invalid directory", try entering WIN and pressing [Enter] again.

The command CD WINDOWS produces another error message. This probably means Windows isn't installed on your computer, or isn't in a directory named Windows

Install Windows (if you have a set of original Windows diskettes), or find out where Windows is installed.

You can't find an icon for the Excel group in the Windows Program Manager. Either there is no Excel group or Excel isn't installed on your PC

First try opening the **File** menu and selecting **Run...**, enter "EXCEL" in the Run window's text box, and click [OK]. If Excel doesn't start at this point, it probably needs to be installed on your system.

No Excel window appears when you start the application. Excel has most likely started out minimized into an icon

Look for the Excel icon. (You might have to minimize the Program Manager window if it's covering everything else.) Double-click the Excel icon to open its window.

The Excel window is too small after startup

Enlarge it by clicking the triangle pointing up on the button at the right edge of the window's title bar. This maximizes the Excel application window to full-screen size.

Chapter 4

Creating A Sample Worksheet

Open Excel and work along with the instructions in this chapter. This will make everything easier to understand. When you start Excel, the application window is open.

 If the window is too small or not visible, you have to maximize it first. If it's already maximized, you'll only see a button with a double-triangle in the upper-right corner of the screen. You should only have to maximize the Excel window once, because your changes are saved whenever you exit the program.

Use the Minimize and Maximize buttons to make the window larger or smaller, or to restore it.

If you can't even find the window, look for an Excel icon along your screen's lower edge, possibly hidden by the Program Manager. Click the triangle pointing down to turn the Program Manager into an icon so you can locate the Excel icon.

QUICK TIP

> Always maximize the Excel application window, so you have as much room as possible for your worksheets.

The Different Areas of Excel and How to Get There

After you start Excel, you'll see the Excel application window and the workbook window displayed on the screen. The workbook window is the most important area of Excel, displaying the workbook you're currently using.

4 | Creating A Sample Worksheet

A worksheet is divided into rows and columns composed of cells. Look closely at your worksheet window for thin lines marking these divisions.

There's also a lettered button at the top of each column to identify the different columns. The rows are numbered along the spreadsheet's left edge.

TAKE NOTE

> By the way, each worksheet starts out being the same size, with 256 columns and 16384 rows. You'll probably never need this much space, but you should know Excel's limits anyway. Any cells you don't use remain empty and, when you save the worksheet, only the occupied cells are saved.

Selecting a cell

Before you can enter any information in a cell, you have to select the cell. Just click it with your mouse pointer. The selected cell will have a border around it, and its coordinates will be displayed at the left edge of the formula bar.

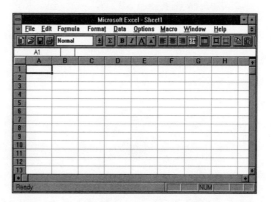

An example of a selected cell

Anything you enter in this cell will also be displayed in the formula bar. The formula bar shows the coordinates of the selected cell and its contents.

QUICK TIP

> Your mouse pointer changes its appearance when it's in the formula bar.

Selecting cells outside the visible worksheet segment

Excel has several ways to move through the worksheet and select a cell, even if you can't see it yet. Each worksheet has approximately 4,000,000 cells that are outside the screen area. The secret to selecting one of these cells is to first make that cell visible. You can either use the scroll bars or Excel's special movement buttons.

To view other parts of the worksheet, use the scroll bars on the right side and bottom of the worksheet window. These take you from side to side and up and down. The easiest way to do this is to click the arrow buttons at either end of the scroll bars. Note the button in the middle of each scroll bar; this shows where you are relative to the whole worksheet horizontally or vertically.

Place the mouse pointer on a scroll button and drag the button in the direction you want to go. When you reach the right place, release the mouse button. Now Excel displays your new position.

The worksheet is moving - what's going on?

Suppose you just made a selection and you're dragging the selection to another location in the worksheet. You reach the right edge or lower edge of the worksheet window and continue to drag the selection beyond that. Suddenly, it appears that the worksheet is moving.

Actually, you're just shifting the visible portion of the worksheet as you move through it with the selection. You can see the action being recorded by the column or row coordinates, as they change rapidly to keep track of the changing location. You finally stop moving when you reach the farthest column, IV, or the farthest row, 16384.

Creating A Sample Worksheet

What's really disorienting about this process is that you lose track of cells you want to see, when your worksheet moves out of their display range. Don't worry; you can return to your former position any time.

> Don't panic or become frustrated if you feel like you're lost in your worksheet. Simply press Ctrl + Home to go to cell A1. You can then return to your original position from this cell.

QUICK TIP

Moving through the worksheet with the keyboard

Your keyboard's cursor keys come in handy here. You can jump right to cell A1 by pressing Ctrl + Home . Pressing only Home lets you jump to the first cell of the column you're in.

Entering Numbers in Your Worksheets

The formula bar

Once you select a cell, you can enter numbers and other information in it. You activate the worksheet's formula bar as soon as you begin to type. There are two buttons in the formula bar when it's active.

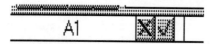

Everything you enter in the formula bar also appears in the cell. This lets you enter information as well as edit it. Once you're satisfied with your entry, you have two ways to confirm it (so the computer knows that's what you want in the cell):

- Click the button with the checkmark in the formula bar.

- Press Enter and then press a cursor key. This moves the selection border to the next cell (to the left or right, or up or down, depending on which arrow you used).

QUICK TIP

> When entering information in a cell, always watch the formula bar. That's where you have control. The cell information shouldn't distract you.

The red cancel box in the formula bar

The other button in the formula bar has a red X called a cancel box on it. You use this to abort, or stop, an action you just took. Say you enter something, then realize you don't want it. Click the red cancel box and your entry disappears. Another way to abort an action is to press Esc.

Seeing double

Be careful not to watch the cell as it displays what you enter in the formula bar. You really only have control over the contents of the formula bar.

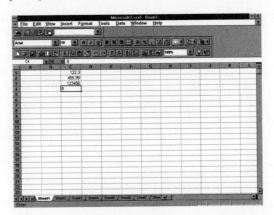

Seeing double?

Entering lengthy number sequences

You can enter long sequences of numbers quickly in Excel much the same way you would on a calculator with adding tape. With a calculator, you place one hand on the keypad and use your other hand to follow the list of numbers you have to enter. In Excel, it's only a little different.

33

Creating A Sample Worksheet

Use your mouse pointer to click the first cell in column C, cell C1. If you aren't sure you selected the right cell, press Ctrl + Home to jump directly to cell A1, then press the right arrow key twice to reach cell C1. Now enter a number with as many digits as you want from the numeric keypad; you can include a decimal point or a negative number (with a minus sign in front of it). However don't enter commas to separate the thousands and don't enter dollar signs or other currency symbols.

> A basic rule for entering numbers in Excel cells is to keep them as plain as possible. That's why you usually won't enter the commas or dollar signs.

QUICK TIP

	A	B	C	D
1			122.3	
2			455.99	
3			123456	
4			8	
5			46.22	
6			89,333	
7			465	
8			65465	
9			55,222	
10			45	
11			-45	
12			-99999.999	
13			7.89E+18	
14				

Number columns

Correcting mistakes

As long as the formula bar remains active, you may modify your entry. For instance, you can use Backspace to delete characters to the left of the cursor.

You can click any place in the formula bar where you want to enter or delete characters. The cursor will automatically go there. Every character you enter is inserted at the cursor location.

If you click the blank area to the right of the formula bar, the cursor goes beyond the last character in the formula bar.

Since you want to enter numbers quickly, type the number on your numeric keypad and press (Enter). This deactivates the formula bar and the two buttons (green checkmark and red cancel box) disappear.

Now you can enter information in another cell. Remember, when you begin to type a number, letter, punctuation, or special character, you reactivate the formula bar for whatever cell you selected. Try typing several numbers for several cells, and you'll see how fast and simple it is. Make certain you press a cursor key to move to the next cell.

WARNING!

> Make certain the cell you selected is empty before you start typing. If you select a cell with information in it, and you type something in the formula bar, the new information replaces the cell's previous information. If you press (Enter), you permanently replace the old entry with the new. However, if you haven't pressed (Enter) yet, you can click the red cancel box button or press (Esc) to undo any damage.

What does E+ or ######## mean?

You might find something strange when you enter a large number in an Excel cell. To illustrate, select cell D1 and enter 999999999999 (twelve nines), then press (Enter).

When you enter a number that's too big for the cell, Excel shows the number as either ######## or 1E+12. Excel is saying the number is too large to fit into the cell. (The "1E+12" is Excel's way of trying to display it in a different format.)

If you reactivate this cell's formula bar by re-selecting the cell, 999999999999 will reappear. Excel just represented the actual number with ######## or 1E+12.

Creating A Sample Worksheet

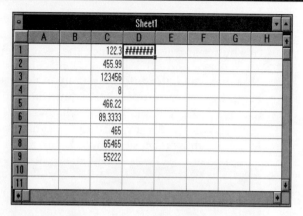

######## means your entry doesn't fit in the cell

Don't believe what you see

Here again you've encountered one of Excel's basic rules: The contents of a cell and the way these contents are displayed aren't always the same. However, how can you get Excel to show the actual number in the cell? You need to increase the size of the cell so it's wide enough to show the whole number. However, it's impossible to widen only one cell; you need to widen the entire column.

Solution - column widening

Back to our illustration: Move your mouse pointer to the area containing the column coordinates. As you move the pointer, watch it carefully. When it crosses the border between columns D and E, it becomes a vertical line with horizontal arrows on the left and right.

Grab this border line and drag it to the right, then release the mouse button. You've just widened Column D. If you widened it enough, Excel should be able to display 999999999999 in the cell. If not, just grab this border again and drag it to the right a little more.

The format of a number determines how it is displayed in the cell. When you select a certain number format, among the things you determine are the number of decimal places shown and whether there are any leading zeros. You'll find more detailed information on this topic in Chapter 10.

However, this has nothing to do with why Excel displays 999999999999 as 1E+12. This unusual format is called scientific notation. Excel uses this system whenever the number exceeds a certain value although not necessarily when the cell is too small to display it.

Select the same cell and replace the 12-digit number with a smaller one, 9999999999 (eight nines). The following figure shows what you just did:

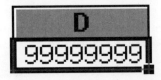

Normal display of numbers

After you widen the column, the number is displayed "correctly".

If Excel displays your number as ########, simply widen the column to give it room to fit. If Excel displays your number in scientific notation, there's nothing you can do.

QUICK TIP

Replacing by overwriting

In the previous example, we said you could replace the 12-digit number with a 10-digit number. When you want to enter something new in a cell, you can just enter new information in that cell's formula bar and Excel automatically replaces the old information with the new. Although that may sound easy, it's also very easy to accidentally delete or change some information.

Creating A Sample Worksheet

Now we're going to replace the information you entered in the worksheet's cells in previous exercises. This example is about recording all the strikes, spares, and gutter balls made by a local bowling league. A very simple worksheet will hold and subsequently evaluate the results of this information.

Let's assume the league has nine members. This worksheet is being created toward the end of the league year and they already made several strikes, spares, and gutter balls. Column C, cells 1 through 9, will contain the values for the individual members for the "spares" category.

Overwriting cell contents

Select cell C1 and click the cell with the cross-shaped mouse pointer. A border now surrounds this cell, and the left side of the formula bar shows the coordinates. Next to these coordinates, the cell's current contents are listed.

NERD TALK

> A cell's coordinates are also called the cell's "reference". The reference of the selected cell in this example is C1.

Type the number 27. The moment you begin to type this number, the formula bar becomes active and "2" appears in the formula bar. Confirm your entry one of the following ways:

- Click the button with the green checkmark in the formula bar. This deactivates the formula bar, but the selection border doesn't move.

- Press Enter.

- Press a cursor key, moving the border to the next cell.

You can immediately enter a value in the next cell. So you probably want to use the second or third option if you're entering a list of numbers. For our exercise, repeat this process in cells C2 through cell C9, entering numbers between 3 and 30. If you had entered values in cell C10 or beyond, don't bother to delete the contents. Just ignore them for now.

Now go to column B and enter similar values in cells B1 through B9; these are the team's strikes. Do the same in column D, with references D1 through D9, recording gutter balls. The numbers for this column should probably be lower, perhaps 1 through 15, to keep the worksheet realistic. When you're done, your worksheet should look something like the following:

	A	B	C	D	E
1		27	27	3	
2		15	9	6	
3		13	12	2	
4		24	14	6	
5		20	29	2	
6		9	15	7	
7		2	4	12	
8		3	17	10	
9		11	8	5	
10					
11					

Bowling worksheet

This is the bowling worksheet with the first nine values in columns B through D.

Entering Text in Your Worksheets

In the first column of the worksheet, you need to enter the bowling league members' names. Enter this text the same way you entered the numbers in the other three columns:

1. Move to cell A1.

2. Type the first name; how about Mark?

3. Confirm the entry and move on to cell A2. Enter the next league member's name.

4. Repeat these steps until you reach cell A9.

4 | Creating A Sample Worksheet

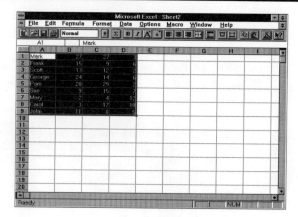

Entering names

This is a worksheet listing the names of the league members in the first nine cells of column A.

This looks great. Unfortunately, we forgot to add column headings. You need these so you don't confuse your gutter balls with your strikes. The following method may be crude, but it's good practice in creating titles for cell contents.

Adding column headings

Eventually, you'll enter column titles in your worksheet; the following exercise makes the space available for these titles. You'll move all the cells down one row, then the titles will go in the top row. The easiest way to do this is to use Excel's cut and paste features.

Select cell A1 by moving the mouse pointer to that cell and clicking the left mouse button. Or press Ctrl + Home for the same effect. Then press and hold the left mouse button while dragging the pointer to cell D9. The selected cells will be displayed in inverse colors.

Select **Cut** from the **Edit** menu. You may also cut the selected cells by pressing Ctrl + X.

Preparing to cut the selected cells

The border of the cut cells is shown as a dashed line.

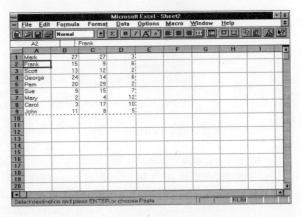

Moved cells

Move to cell A2 and press the left mouse button to select that cell. Paste the cells you cut back into the worksheet by pressing Ctrl + V or by selecting **Paste** from the **Edit** menu (or by pressing Enter). You've moved the cells to the new location.

Creating A Sample Worksheet

Now you're ready to enter the column headings:

1. Move to cell B1, type "Strikes", then press the right arrow key.

2. In cell C1, type "Spares", then press the right arrow key again.

3. In cell D1, type "Gutters", then press Enter.

Your worksheet now looks something like the following:

	A	B	C	D
1		Strikes	Spares	Gutters
2	Mark	27	27	
3	Frank	15	9	
4	Scott	13	12	
5	George	24	14	
6	Pam	20	29	
7	Sue	9	15	
8	Mary	2	4	
9	Caerol	3	17	
10	John	11	8	

Bowling worksheet with column headings

Finding text that's hidden by other text

In cell A1, enter the heading for the contents of column A: Our Bowling League Members' Names. After you enter this title, compare the text in the formula bar with that in the cell. The text appears acceptable in the formula bar, but only part of it is displayed in the cell. Although you could press the Enter key, the cell only displays the text that fits; the rest is simply cut off.

This happens because Excel treats text differently than numbers. Since you don't have to use text in subsequent calculations, it can exceed the cell's width. However, one long piece of text might cover another.

Using our example to illustrate, the word "Strikes" in cell B1 covers the remaining text in cell A1. You can increase the cell's width to show the whole title for A1. However, that column would be very wide and we'll make other changes to our bowling worksheet later anyway. So we won't want you to do this. Instead, replace the lengthy title with something shorter, like "Names".

Correcting Typos

Did you type all the names correctly the first time? Then you've done quite well. We can't say the same, because our fingers stumbled when we typed Carol. We mistakenly entered Caerol.

Correcting mistakes in text

A typing mistake is as easy to correct as number typos. You just need to get the cell's contents back in the formula bar. Move to the cell with the typo, then click the formula bar with your mouse. The formula bar automatically displays the cell contents; just click the typo. As soon as the mouse pointer is moved over the formula bar, it changes its appearance to become an I-shaped vertical line, known as an I-beam.

NERD TALK

You find this I-beam mouse pointer in many Windows applications where you enter text. It's different from the text cursor, however. The text cursor indicates where your next character entry will appear; the I-beam just lets you relocate the text cursor. Click an empty box with it and the text cursor appears at the left edge, then you can begin typing your text. When you enter the text, you'll want to move the I-beam out of the area so you can see what you're typing.

Position the I-beam between the incorrect character and the next character to the right. Click the mouse button, and the blinking text cursor appears. Now correct the error: Press Backspace to delete the incorrect character, then enter the correct character.

Creating A Sample Worksheet

When you're done making corrections, click the green checkmark or press [Enter] to confirm the updated cell contents. Now Carol's name is entered correctly.

Selecting Several Cells at Once

It's important to select the cell or cells you want to work with before you perform any operations. The basic Windows rule of thumb is always "first select, then operate". We'll refer to this rule throughout the book because it's a good reminder.

You often need to select several cells at once. For instance, you might need to change an entire range of the worksheet. Or you might want to modify the appearance of several cells at once. We think this is the most simple method for selecting a range:

- Place the mouse pointer on the first cell of the range you want to select.

- Drag the mouse pointer to the last cell of the range.

The selected cells should all be in black, with any information in the cells displayed in white. This is called inverse type.

What is inverse?

Inverse means that the color scheme is reversed: The background is now the type color, and the type is now the background color. On a monochromatic screen, the black-on-white display is inverse, showing white on black. If your PC has a color monitor, you can make the cell background one color and the character in the cell another. You might choose blue type on a yellow background. When you select a cell, the type becomes yellow and the background becomes blue.

Cells as inverse type

Reversing a selection

Here's the really confusing part: The cell you started in when you made the group selection isn't displayed as inverse. The only way you know it's part of a group selection is that the selection border now surrounds all the cells in the selection instead of just the starting cell.

If you want to undo, or unselect, this range, simply click another cell. The selection won't be inverse anymore, and the selection border will surround the cell you clicked.

Selecting entire rows and columns

A worksheet column can be up to 16384 lines and, if you need to select all the cells in a really long column, it would take a long time using the method we just discussed. So we have a shortcut method. Select all the cells in a column, even the ones you can't see on your worksheet at the time, by clicking the button with the desired column coordinate.

The same can be done with rows. Click the button with the row coordinate to select all the cells in that row.

It's also easy to select several columns or rows at once. Simply click the first column or row coordinate and drag the mouse pointer over the next column or row coordinate button. This extends the selection to as many columns or rows as you want.

Creating A Sample Worksheet

Extending selections

When you select more than one column or row, you can only extend the selection in one direction. For example, if you start the selection with column B, you can only extend that selection to column A or to column C and beyond, not in both the left and right directions at once.

So, make sure that you start an extended selection with the first column or row in the group you want before you begin dragging the mouse.

The same goes for selecting ranges. Depending on the starting cell's location, you can drag your selection either to the lower-right, lower-left, upper-right, or upper-left. If you make a selection in one direction, then cross the starting cell to continue the selection, you essentially unselect the preceding cells. The selection is made when you release the mouse button.

> The term "range" is an Excel term referring to selecting several adjacent cells at once. You can describe a range by its reference format (e.g., A1:D1), or you can give them their own names. We'll discuss ranges in more detail in Chapter 5.

NERD TALK

If you want to select all 4,194,304 cells of the worksheet at once, simply click the button in the upper-left corner of the worksheet, where the column and row coordinates intersect. This button contains no text.

The following exercise lets you practice selecting several cells at once. The goal is to change the titles in cells A1 through D1 to bold:

1. Position your mouse pointer on cell A1.

2. Drag the mouse pointer to cell D1. The cells you pass over now appear in inverse type.

3. Release the mouse button. You've now selected the range of cells A1 to D1.

What is the toolbar?

Below the menu bar is a grey bar. Notice the different icons on the grey bar. This is called the toolbar. Like all buttons, each one of these icons triggers a certain action. Symbols on the icon buttons explain the function of each icon.

You can basically accomplish the same functions with these buttons as you can with the menu commands. For example, the icon with a bold "B" changes characters to bold.

When you click one of these buttons with your mouse pointer, you see the icon's effect on the text in your selected cell or cells. The button also tells you it's activated because it now looks like someone pressed it.

This is especially helpful when it's hard to see what's been changed in your cell or range; just glance at the toolbar and you'll know for sure. We'll illustrate this using the bold font toolbar button:

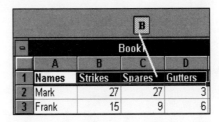

Selected range and "B" toolbar button

By clicking the bold toolbar button, the selected range is assigned a bold font.

By the way, the selection remains active even after you're done. So it's easy to reverse the bold font or whatever change you've made by re-selecting the cell or range and reclicking the icon button.

Deleting What You Don't Want

Obviously, it's important to learn about deleting cell contents. Excel has a simple way to delete a cell, similar to the way you correct typos or overwrite cell contents. We'll use cell A1 to show you the method:

1. Select cell A1.

2. Press `Backspace`, activating the formula bar and making it blank. This effectively empties the cell.

3. Click the green checkmark or press `Enter` to confirm the empty formula bar.

The cell contents have now been deleted, and the cell is as empty as it was to start with.

Deleting several cells at once

It's as easy to delete several cells at once. Select a range of cells and press `Del`.

The range remains selected, but the cells are now empty.

Correcting a deleting mistake

If you accidentally deleted something, you may retrieve it if you can reverse your most recent action. Excel has a menu command that allows you to do this. First open the **Edit** menu. Then click the top command, **Undo**, and Excel restores the cell contents to the selected cells. A shortcut method is simply to press `Ctrl` + `Z`.

Undo reverses your most recent action, whenever such an action is possible. The command you just executed is displayed in the menu, so you can check whether you're actually reversing the right action.

It is even easier to reverse an unintentional deletion in a single cell. When you press `Backspace`, the formula bar is activated. Don't select the `Enter` button however; ask yourself if you really want to delete this cell's contents.

If not, don't confirm the formula bar; instead, click the button with the red cancel box or simply press ⌊Esc⌋. Then the deletion is canceled and the cell's previous contents are restored.

Different Ways to Add

Until now, you've experimented with Excel's worksheets by following our examples. Now we want to discuss the main reason you use Excel: Worksheet calculations. We'll start with addition.

In the bowling worksheet, add all the members' strikes, spares, and gutter balls. Cell B11 should contain the sum of the numbers in cells B2 to B10. Think about how to solve this problem with a calculator: Simply enter the first number, press "+", enter the next number, press "+" again, and so on.

You solve this in Excel in almost the same way. The difference is that you won't have to recalculate the series if any of the numbers on the worksheet change, because Excel will store your calculation.

The following example explains this:

1. Move to cell B11.

2. Start by entering an equal sign (=). This tells Excel something is being calculated and the result will appear in this cell.

3. Begin entering the contents to be added. Instead of using the values in the cells, use each cell's reference to identify it. The first entry will be reference B2.

> It doesn't matter whether the column reference letter is in upper or lowercase when you enter it.

QUICK TIP

4. Enter a plus (+) sign to connect the first value with the next one.

5. Type the next reference, B3, then another plus sign.

6. Type the next cell reference, B4, then another plus sign.

Creating A Sample Worksheet

7. Continue this for the remaining cells. Do not add a plus sign after the last cell reference, B10.

Ultimately, you should see the following in your formula bar:

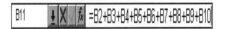

Summation formula

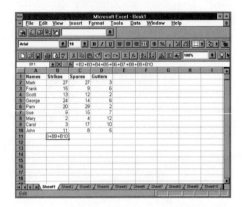

Sum within the cell

After you've confirmed this entry by pressing [Enter], the result immediately appears in cell B11. Is the sum correct? Move to B11 again. Look at what you entered in this formula bar: =B2+B3+B4+B5+B6+B7+B8+B9+B10. This is called a formula. Excel calculated this formula and wrote the result in cell B11.

By the way, if you used the lowercase "b" in entering your formula, notice how Excel converted each to uppercase letters.

Formulas add flexibility

If you had manually added the numbers in B2 through B10 and entered the total in B11, Excel couldn't recalculate the total for you if any of the numbers changed. However, by adding the numbers in a formula like this, Excel can automatically recalculate. You can try this by replacing the value in cell B2 with 1000. Confirm the entry in the formula bar by pressing [Enter], then watch how the result in cell B11 changes.

Excel recognizes a cell's formula by the mathematical operator that you enter. The (=) sign in cell B11 is one of these. They also include (+) for addition, (-) for subtraction, (*) for multiplication, (/) for division, and (^) for exponentials. Glance at your keyboard's keypad for these keys.

Mathematical operations are conducted in a specific order. To change the way a formula is evaluated, use parentheses. For example, the following formula

```
=2^8*9+78
```

is evaluated as 2382. Adding a set of parentheses, the same set of numbers

```
=2^8*(9+78)
```

is evaluated as 22,272. Moving the parentheses around, this set of numbers

```
=2^(8*9)+78
```

is evaluated as a gigantic number that Excel has to display as 4.72E+21.

Semi-automatic addition

Now imagine you have to add a column of 324 numbers. Doing it the way we just described would really take considerable time. Excel lets you save time and patience with functions which let you specify what to calculate. For adding cell contents, for example, Excel has the SUM function.

To illustrate, delete the contents of cell B11, then:

1. Enter an equal sign (=) to tell Excel you're entering a formula.

2. Enter the word SUM after the equal sign. Remember that it doesn't matter whether you use upper or lowercase letters.

3. Enter an open parentheses after the word SUM.

4. Enter the references of the first and last cells in the range to be added: B2:B10. This information stands for "all cells from B2 to B10".

5. Enter a closing parenthesis. Your formula bar should look like this: "=sum(b2:b10)". Confirm it by pressing (Enter).

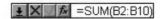

SUM function

The result is identical to the previous sum, but your formula is much shorter.

Notice there is a different formula in cell B11. This method really helps reduce the amount of typing.

Fully-automatic addition

Excel automatically calculates sums. Try this out using the sum for our league's spares in cells C2 through C10:

1. Move to cell C11.

2. Select the range from C11 to C2, by dragging your mouse pointer over these cells or holding down (Shift) while pressing (↑) until you reach cell C2.

3. Click the (Autosum) button in the toolbar, which looks like the icon to the right. The formula bar is activated automatically, and displays the formula "=SUM(C2:C10)".

That's about as simple as it gets. You can now try this approach with the cells in column D.

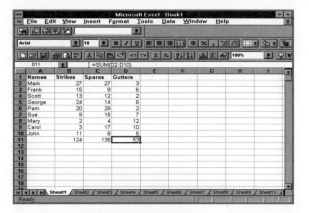

The SUM function

Lasting Values - Saving the Worksheet

The information stored in RAM is lost when the computer is switched off. Until now, all the work we did in our worksheet has been stored in the computer's RAM.

You need to store the worksheet so you can retrieve it and make changes later. Your computer's hard drive is the perfect place to store it.

NERD TALK

> RAM is a computer term meaning Random Access Memory. This is the part of your computer that stores information while you're working with it. To run Windows, you probably have at least 2 megabytes of RAM. Many modern computers have much more than this available.

Unlike your computer's memory, the hard drive retains all its information even when the computer is switched off. A hard drive can contain a lot of information, but it has to store it in some organized way.

4 | Creating A Sample Worksheet

You can save your bowling worksheet whenever you want to take a break, but you have to name it first. You can give it an original name, or use the one Excel gave it when you first started working in it, Sheet1. This name is displayed in the bowling worksheet's title bar.

Saving your worksheet as a file

Open the **File** menu and click **Save** to open the "Save As" dialog box. Warning: this may be very confusing at first glance.

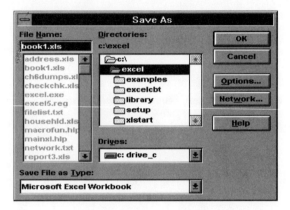

The Save dialog box

In the upper-left corner is a text box labeled "File Name:" and, in it, the official name of your workbook is listed, BOOK1.XLS. Excel automatically adds the ".XLS" to identify it as an Excel workbook file.

Folders and directories

On the right side of the dialog box is a list box called "Directories:". This displays the directories on the hard drive. The directory displayed here is the one your worksheet will be filed in. If you want to file it in another directory, you need to change the one displayed here.

Each directory has a name so you can identify it, and this one is "c:\winapps\excel". Your directory may be "c:\excel" or something similar. There are other directories listed below this one, each with what looks like a closed folder. Your directory has what looks like an open folder and it's in another color.

Opening a directory

You can choose to store the worksheet in a different directory. To practice, click the "example" directory listed beneath the "excel" one. This selected the entire line this icon is on. Click OK in the upper-right corner of the dialog box and check out what's changed. The "examples" folder is now open and in a different color. The "excel" folder is closed and displayed in the color of the other closed folders (yellow). Above the list is now a line something like:

```
c:\excel\examples
```

This is where your worksheet will now be saved.

Renaming your worksheet

You can also change your worksheet's name to something else. Using our example worksheet, let's call it BOWLING. Move your mouse pointer over the text box, "File Name:" and watch it turn into an I-beam. Click the space just after the letter "S" and a blinking text cursor appears. Delete the current file name using Backspace, then enter the new name:

```
bowling
```

Once again, Excel makes no distinction between upper and lowercase letters.

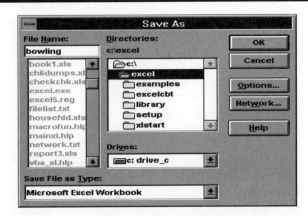

Renaming a worksheet

CAUTION!

> The file name has to be eight characters or less and cannot contain spaces. Stick with letters, numbers and, perhaps, dashes for the name.

Click OK in this dialog box; the worksheet will be saved under the name BOWLING.XLS and stored in the directory C:\EXCEL\EXAMPLE on your hard drive. It doesn't take very long for the computer to save the file and, when it's done, your worksheet's new file name is displayed in the title bar.

When You're Ready to Quit

Closing the worksheet

Now that you saved your worksheet, you can close it. Select **Close** from the **File** menu and Excel immediately executes your command, if you didn't make any changes to the worksheet since you saved it. If you did, Excel displays a message before the worksheet is closed that looks like this:

File close message

If you try to save your worksheet without saving the most recent changes, Excel displays a "Save changes" message.

Click [Yes] to confirm this question, and Excel saves your worksheet again. Then it automatically closes the file.

Quitting Excel

Without an open worksheet window, Excel looks pretty bare. You can open another worksheet if you want to, but let's say you just want to leave Excel. Use **Exit** in the **File** menu to close the Excel application window and return to the Windows Program Manager. If you want to switch off your computer, you have to quit Windows too. When the C:\> prompt appears, switch off your PC.

> If you want to switch off your computer now, you have to first close the Windows user interface. This ensures that any changes you've made to Windows are saved. Select **Exit Windows...** from the Program Manager's **File** menu. Windows displays a dialog box where you need to click [OK].

CAUTION!

Starting Excel and opening the worksheet

Now you're ready to resume working on the bowling workbook. Switch on your computer and open the Windows user interface. Then go into the Program Manager and double-click the Excel icon to start Excel.

To find out more about starting your PC, refer to Chapter 3.

4 | Creating A Sample Worksheet

When Excel starts, it automatically opens the application window and a new workbook window. Go into the **File** menu and open your bowling workbook. It will be listed as a command and you just need to double-click it to open the workbook.

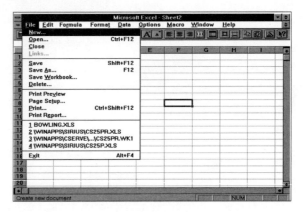

The File menu

The **File** menu lists the most recently saved workbooks as commands so you can open them directly.

Opening older worksheets

The **File** menu only lists the last four worksheets you saved. If you want to modify a worksheet that isn't listed here, you need to select it from a dialog box. Select **Open...** from your **File** menu and you'll see the "Open" dialog box, structured like the one you used when you saved a worksheet. Make certain the workbook you're looking for is listed in the "File Name:" text box.

All you probably see is the abbreviation *.XL*, indicating that this only includes files with this extension. This makes a lot of sense, since Excel always gives workbooks the "XLS" extension when it saves them. However, you won't necessarily see your bowling workbook (named BOWLING.XLS) in the file list now, because Excel always starts with the "c:\excel" directory open. You'll also see that the Excel folder icon is displayed in a different color and appears opened.

If you saved your workbook in a different directory, you need to get into that directory first. We saved the bowling worksheet in the EXAMPLE directory, which is listed below "c:\excel". Open this directory by selecting it and clicking OK. Look through the file list, which now displays all the worksheets in the EXAMPLE directory, and click on BOWLING.XLS. It's transferred into the "File Name:" text box and will be opened when you click OK again.

Problems Creating A Worksheet

Below we mention many of the problems you could encounter while setting up a worksheet. We discuss the solutions for each of these problems and, in some cases, we discuss them further. Some of the things we mention have already been worked out in this chapter.

My work area is too small

If the Excel window is too small when you first get into the application, simply click the button with the triangle pointing up, located at the right end of the application window's title bar.

The Minimize and Maximize buttons are in the application window's title bar.

You should do this regardless of your window size, to be sure the window is maximized. When you finish in Excel, all the changes you made to the application window are also saved. Now, when you go back into Excel, it will look exactly the same as when you left it.

QUICK TIP

You can also maximize a workbook window, which we recommend, so you'll have maximum workspace. Worksheet windows have two buttons at the right edge of the title bar that allow you to minimize or maximize the window. When you maximize a worksheet window, its title bar disappears and the worksheet name appears in the application window's title bar. When the window is maximized, you'll see a button with a double triangle at the right end of the menu bar. At the left end of the menu bar is a Control-menu box (used to activate the Control menu).

I've gotten lost in my worksheet

This is fairly easy to do, when you're selecting and accessing cells outside of the visible area. You can re-orient yourself by simply jumping back to cell A1. The easiest way to do this is to press Ctrl + Home .

QUICK TIP

If you want to go to a specific cell, access the **Go To...** command from your **Edit** menu. It opens a dialog box with a text box labeled "Reference:". The text cursor is already blinking in this text box, so you only need to type the cell reference (e.g., H99). Click OK to jump to the cell. A shortcut to accessing **Goto...** is to press the F5 function key.

The visible portion of my worksheet shifts while I type

You enter something in a cell that's located at one of the four edges of your worksheet window. As you confirm your entry, the entire visible portion of the worksheet shifts. Cells you may still need might disappear from the screen. The only way to solve this is to deliberately use cursor keys to confirm your entries. If the cell is located at the lower edge of the screen, use ↑; at the right edge, use ←; and at the left edge, use →.

QUICK TIP

> If you want to see a specific portion of the worksheet, use the scroll bars. These shift the worksheet's visible portion up or down, or left or right. You can keep your bearings by watching the scroll button in each scroll bar, which tells you where you are relative to the whole worksheet.

I'm typing in the formula bar, but it doesn't appear in the cell

Are you sure you confirmed your entry? Once you type the cell contents in the formula bar, you can either click the button with the green checkmark, press (Enter), or press one of the cursor keys. Any of these actions lets Excel know this is what you want in the cell. If you enter something, then click the button with the red cancel box or press (Esc) by mistake, Excel simply ignores the characters you entered.

I entered a number, but Excel's displaying a lot of symbols

The number you enter is displayed the way you entered it, if the cell is wide enough. If it's too large for the cell, Excel may display it as ########. To solve this problem, you have to widen the column.

Remember that your mouse pointer changes appearance when you move it over the border between columns. Grab the border with your mouse pointer and drag your mouse to the right, then release the button. The column is now wider than before; just make certain it's wide enough to display the number correctly.

QUICK TIP

> You can increase or decrease the width of any column this way. Be careful, however, because it can disappear if you decrease it too much. If you notice it right away, immediately select **Undo Column Width** from your **Edit** menu. If you don't notice it until later, try the following steps.

1. Locate the missing column (done most easily by reading off the column letters and seeing which is missing).

2. Select the columns on either side of the missing one: place the mouse pointer on the left-hand column coordinate and drag it to the right-hand column coordinate.

3. Select **Column Width...** from your **Format** menu.

4. Click "Standard width" and confirm by clicking OK.

This makes the missing column as wide as the adjacent columns, so the missing one "appears" again.

When you enter extremely large numbers, Excel displays them in scientific notation such as 1E+12. The only way to solve this problem is to change the number's format.

Chapter 10 discusses number display in greater detail.

The text I entered is covered up

Excel treats text differently than numbers. You can enter as much text as you like in a cell and, if the cell or cells to the right of the text cell are empty, your text will be displayed. However, if there is information in a cell to the right of the text cell, it will be shown "on top of" the remaining text. There isn't any way to remedy this problem directly, but we suggest that you try to shorten the text so it can fit.

I can't figure out which cells I selected

You selected a range of cells, but they don't all appear as inverse, so you aren't sure whether they're all selected. Normally, the starting cell doesn't appear as inverse, but it is contained in the border surrounding the whole range.

QUICK TIP

> If several non-adjacent cells are selected, you may have pressed Ctrl while you moved to one of these cells. Ctrl lets you select a non-adjacent range of cells. To unselect this assortment, simply click any other cell and this will reverse any previous selection.

I can't tell whether this text is bold

Say you experimented with assigning a bold font to text cells; now you can't remember which are bold and which aren't. All you need to do is select a cell then see if the bold toolbar button (the one with the letter B) looks like it's pressed down.

QUICK TIP

> This also applies to other attributes of cell contents. Chapter 7 has further information on different icons.

Why can't I use [Backspace] *to delete several cells at once?*

You selected a range so you can delete all its cells. However, when you pressed [Backspace], the contents of the range's starting cell (the one that's not displayed as inverse) were deleted. To delete the contents of all the cells in the range, you need to press [Del].

How can I give my workbook its own name?

When you open a blank workbook, Excel has already given it a default name consisting of the word, "Book", and a number. If you want to assign your own name, you just need to save it.

Select **Save** from your **File** menu, which opens a dialog box. In this box, specify the name of the workbook, under "File Name:", and the directory in which you want it stored.

Remember, the file name has to be eight characters or less and can only contain letters, numbers, and hyphens. Excel automatically adds the ".XLS" extension to identify the file as an Excel workbook.

I don't know how to find and load a workbook

You usually need to know the workbook's name and where it's located before you can go looking for it. If it's one of the four most recently saved workbooks, it appears as a command in the **File** menu. You can open one of these workbooks directly by double-clicking on the file's name.

Creating A Sample Worksheet

If it's older, you have to click **Open** in the **File** menu, which opens a dialog box. Here you enter the file name in the text box on the left, then click (OK) to open the workbook.

If you don't know the file's name, you can open the directory it's in, then search the list of files in that directory. Choose the directory from the list box on the right-hand side of the dialog box, then click (OK). In the left-hand side list box, find the worksheet and click on it, then click (OK) to open the worksheet.

Chapter 5

Creating Worksheets

In Chapter 4 you worked on creating a simple workbook and learned that a workbook can contain several million different numbers. Although you probably won't use this, you'll often build larger and more complex workbooks. This chapter explores many ways to simplify your work with large workbooks and familiarizes you with the complicated functions for evaluating numbers in a workbook. To give you some hands-on experience, start by creating a new workbook.

Closing the Old Workbook, Opening a New One

You don't even need to close the workbook you're working on to start a new one. Excel can manage a large number of workbook windows in its application window. However, it's usually best to close any workbooks you no longer need. There are two ways to close a workbook window and its workbook:

- Double-click the **Control** menu (the square with the dash at the left side of the title bar)

or

- Select **Close** from the **File** menu.

If you haven't made any changes since you last saved the workbook, Excel closes this workbook and its window. If you made changes, Excel displays a warning message. Simply click ⟨Yes⟩ in this dialog box and Excel will save the revised workbook under its current name.

Warning message before closing a workbook

When no workbook windows are open, the Excel menu bar looks empty. Only the **File** menu and the **Help** menu titles are still visible. There are also fewer menu items under **File**. At this point, all you can really do is open an existing workbook or open a new one. The **Exit** command for ending Excel is also in the **File** menu.

Start a new workbook by selecting **New...** from the **File** menu. A new workbook should open. If a dialog box opens, offering you a choice of "Workbook" or "Slides", select "Workbook" and click OK. Usually the "Workbook" entry will be selected as a default. If this entry isn't selected already, click it. Then click OK.

Excel opens a new workbook window for you containing a blank worksheet, complete with a default sheet tab name like Sheet1. The workbook window's title bar will list the workbook under the title Book2 or Book3.

Planning the workbook project

Calling your workbook a project may seem overwhelming, but we believe you need to plan your workbook carefully, especially if it's a large one. Make a pencil sketch of your workbook first. This way you won't cruise aimlessly across the workbook, darting between rows and columns, entering and deleting things. We'll use a household budget for the first project. Let's call it "Household Budget". You should be able to apply this example to work, to track traveling expenses for instance, or in some other way.

First, ask what you want to enter in this workbook and what you want to calculate. For a household budget, you enter information about your income and expenditures, and arrange the information in different categories. We'll want to calculate at least the balance (income minus expenditures) and subtotals for the individual categories.

If you already maintain this type of household budget, use your handwritten version as a model for your Excel workbook. If not, begin by making a pencil sketch of the workbook and include a list of the individual amounts and categories.

Don't bother with the workbook's appearance right now. Chapter 7 examines these fine points of Excel workbooks.

Of course, all this information must be organized. The first column contains the headings for the income, expenditure and balance areas. The second column contains the different categories. The third column contains the different items.

Display the project's name, "Household Budget", in the top row to make everything clear. You might want to include the current year and the family name: "Household Budget 1993 for the Smith family". Display the breakdown of months and weeks in the second row.

Keep a blank row following each area and category for the subtotals.

QUICK TIP

Before you go any further, Maximize the workbook window and save your workbook under a permanent name. Maximizing it gives you maximum workspace. Save the workbook now, so you have one less thing to worry about while you're working on the workbook.

Creating Worksheets

Saving your workbook

Select **Save** from the **File** menu. In this dialog box, open the EXAMPLES directory or another directory in which to store the Household Budget workbook file. Enter the workbook's name under "File name:"; it has to be eight characters or less. We suggest using "Househld". Click OK and Excel saves the workbook under the name "HOUSEHLD.XLS" in the directory you chose. Feel free to confirm this by checking the Excel workbook window's title bar, which displays the new name.

Entering the Workbook Contents

Enter the headings first, starting in cell A1. Move to this cell and enter the name of this project. Any text that doesn't fit in this cell spills over to the cells to the right.

The second row remains blank at this point. Later we'll use it to enter the individual months. In the third row, enter the title for the first area. Move to A3 and type "Expenditures" (or "Income" if you prefer to have this appear above the expenditures). Don't forget to confirm each entry with Enter.

You can probably already tell that setting up a slightly more complex worksheet requires some planning and logical thinking. Column B shows the names for the categories. In cell B3, enter "Fixed expenditures" or any name you want to use to clearly explain the items listed.

In column C3, enter "Rent" or "Mortgage payment". We'll assume this is due monthly.

Placeholders

Move the cell pointer to cell D3, where you need to enter a number. It's likely that you don't know what number to enter here, so we suggest you enter a number that acts as a placeholder for now (the number zero works well). This lets you use this development stage to determine which cells will contain numbers and which will contain something else (words or formulas).

Because you used numbers as placeholders in all the number cells, you make the workbook a lot easier to use. You need to use placeholders because you don't know what values you'll need to enter. Just use zeros in all these cells. You should, however, consider how you want the values to appear when you enter them. In the case of our Household Budget, the values will all be dollar amounts.

Formatting the number cells

Select cell D3 if it isn't currently selected, then choose **Cells...** in the **Format** menu. When the "Format Cells" dialog box opens, click the "Number" tab. The dialog box should look like this:

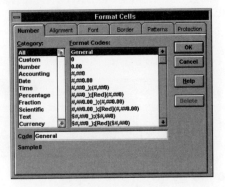

Format Cells dialog box

Number format is briefly discussed in Chapter 4. Also refer to Chapter 10 for a full discussion of this.

The dialog box shows two lists, one called "Category", the other "Format Codes". Excel analyzes a number and automatically determines whether it's an integer, a percent, or even a date. If it can't recognize the number's format, Excel selects "All", displaying all the available number formats.

If the "General" format is selected, Excel processes the number as a value. Large values may be displayed in scientific notation.

Chapter 4 talks more about scientific notation.

Just below "General" is an entry named 0, for integer numbers. Click this entry and it appears in the "Code" text box at the lower edge. Below this, "Sample" shows what the number in the selected cell will look like in the specified format. For 0, nothing changes. However, try 0.00. "Sample" now displays the simple zero as 0.00.

The specified number format determines what the number in the cell will look like. Selecting the number format 0 produces integer numbers. "1.23456789" is displayed as "1". Excel automatically rounds the value to the nearest whole number, so "1.98765432" is displayed as "2".

Select the number format 0.00 for numbers with two decimal places. An integer number is displayed with two trailing zeros. For example, "2" becomes "2.00". Use this format for the Household Budget. Select this number format and close the dialog box by clicking OK.

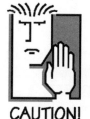

Number formats are discussed in detail in Chapter 10.

CAUTION!

> One number format for currency values, found in the "Currency" category of the dialog box, places a dollar sign ($) in front of every number. This may be more confusing while you're still learning all this, so don't choose this format now.

Copying cells in different ways

Like all applications that run under the Windows user interface, Excel has its own copier. You can use this to copy information from one cell or range and paste it in another location. This copier is called a Clipboard.

Select a cell or range, copy its contents to the Clipboard, then move to the new location and paste the Clipboard information. Excel automatically pastes it in the new cell or range. This operation is identical in all applications that run under Windows. Try it with the following example:

1. Select cell D3 if it isn't already selected.

2. Select **Copy** from the **Edit** menu. A moving dashed border, like a marquee, indicates that the cell's contents have been copied to the Clipboard.

3. Move to cell D4. You can still see the marquee around cell D3, but now it doesn't have the selection border around it.

4. Select **Paste** from the **Edit** menu. A copy of the contents of cell D3 now appears in cell D4.

5. The marquee is still around cell D3, indicating the copy of its contents is still in the Clipboard. To verify this paste the contents into cell D**5**.

In complex worksheets, you might copy and paste repeatedly but there are shortcuts. Excel has a whole range of functions that makes it easy to paste the same copy into several cells at once:

1. Is the marquee still visible around D3? If not, select the cell again and click **Copy** from the **Edit** menu.

2. Move to cell D6.

3. From this cell, press the mouse button and drag the mouse pointer to cell D10, then release the mouse button.

4. Select **Paste** from the **Edit** menu. A copy of this cell's contents appears in each of the selected cells.

Use a shortcut to avoid opening the **Edit** menu twice for simple copying and pasting. First get rid of the marquee, then select this cell and press Enter. Press Ctrl + C and the marquee surrounds the cell again. Look at the lower edge of your application window. You should see a notice about the pasting shortcut:

> Select destination and press ENTER or choose Paste

Move to cell D11 and press Enter. You just pasted a copy of D3 in cell D11. This method has one disadvantage. The copy on the Clipboard is deleted when you paste the contents in the new cell. If you want to paste the contents of D3 in more than one cell, use the previous method.

Creating Worksheets

Filling cells in certain directions

You can also fill a range of cells with the contents of the starting cell. As you may remember, a range's starting cell is active when you begin the range's selection. Experiment with this technique:

1. Move to cell D11, which should contain a zero from a previous copying example.

2. Select the cells below, up to, and including cell D20.

3. Select **Fill/Down** from the **Edit** menu.

All the cells in this range now have the same contents as the starting cell. **Fill/Down** works for filling cells below the starting cell, only in a column. Use **Fill/Right**, also found in your **Edit** menu, to fill a range of cells to the right of the starting cell, only in a row. Avoid these commands if your range is above or to the left of the starting cell.

AutoFill and the fill handle

Excel's AutoFill feature lets you fill cells automatically, using a special tool called a fill handle. Look closely at the border surrounding a selected cell or range. As you can see in the illustration to the right, the fill handle is the small black square at the border's lower-right corner.

Move the mouse pointer onto the fill handle, and the mouse pointer turns into a plus sign (+). Drag the selection border over adjacent cells to copy the starter cell's contents to all the cells you drag across. You can drag only horizontally or vertically, not diagonally.

Before you can test this in your Household Budget, you need to clear some space. Delete all the cells in column D below cell D3:

1. Select D4.

2. Hold down the mouse button and drag the mouse pointer to the last cell containing a zero, D20. Release the mouse button to select the range.

3. Press (Del).

Now practice using the AutoFill feature and the fill handle tool to automatically fill cells:

1. Return to cell D3 and use your mouse pointer to click the selected cell's fill handle. The mouse pointer turns into a plus sign (+).

2. Drag the mouse pointer to cell D50. This stretches a cross-hatched border over the cells you select. The worksheet will shift as you move beyond the window's lower edge.

3. Release the mouse button. The value that you copied appears in all the cells you covered with the border. This range remains selected until you make another selection.

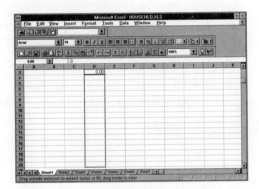

Opening a fill frame

Use AutoFill to enter zeros in other ranges. For practice, go to the selected range's fill handle and drag the mouse pointer to the right. When you reach column O, all the cells for all twelve months will be filled.

Creating Worksheets

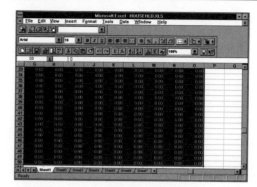

Filled cells

QUICK TIP

AutoFill lets you create all these zeros in just one operation.

> As long as you hold the mouse button down, you can move the mouse pointer back and forth while you select ranges of cells. This lets you determine how far the fill range will extend.

If you feel stranded in the farther recesses of your worksheet, simply press [Ctrl] + [Home] to return to the worksheet's first cell.

Using AutoFill to create a series

You can use AutoFill to create a running series of numbers for your column headings, including rows of dates and times. Practice this on the Household Budget's column headings, where each month has its own column:

1. Type "January" in cell D2.

2. Drag the selection border's fill handle to cell O2.

3. Release the mouse button, and the succeeding months are displayed in the individual cells.

If you release the mouse button before you complete your selection, AutoFill will be executed in only part of the cells. Let's say your index finger gave out around cell J2, July. To fill the remaining cells, click the fill handle at J2 and drag all the way to O2. Now all the cells show the succession of months, from January to December.

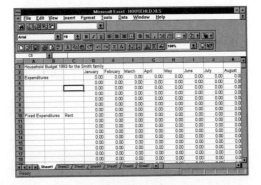

Worksheet with text

Moving cells around the worksheet

Let's assume you mixed up the sequence of your headings. You could delete the whole row of column headings and re-enter them in the correct order. Excel's method is a little less painless. Simply move the cells to their correct locations. Try moving the main title from A1 to B1:

1. Select cell A1. A selection border appears around the cell.

2. Position your mouse pointer exactly on the selection border. The mouse pointer turns into an arrow pointing in the upper-left direction.

3. Grab the selection border and drag the selection frame from A1 to B1, then release the mouse button. The contents of cell A1 are now in cell B1. Drag B3 to A10, and C3 to B10.

You can move ranges of cells this same way.

Changing column width

The items in column A aren't very readable.

1. Select cell A1. Choose **Column/Width...** from the **Format** menu.

2. In the "Column Width:" text box, type the number 16 and press [Enter].

Inserting rows

You still need to include the rows for subtotals. The worksheet is more legible if you include subtotals for each range and category. However, we didn't leave any blank rows open, so you need to insert rows.

You can insert new cells in a worksheet any time. However, you cannot just insert one cell; you need to insert a whole column or row of cells. This is a simple procedure. For the subtotal of the fixed expenditures, we want to insert a row of subtotal cells after all the expenditures have been listed. In our example, this is above row 10. Select this row by clicking its row coordinate, 10, at the left edge of the window.

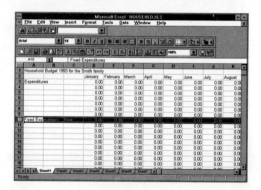

Selecting a row

Now select **Rows** from the **Insert** menu and a new row appears in your worksheet. All the rows below this new one move down one row. You need to decide where to place the row header "Subtotal". Whether you place it in column B or C, be consistent with other subtotal headings. Follow these steps to insert blank rows for subtotals of the other groups.

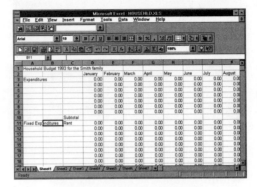

Household Budget worksheet

Formulas

QUICK TIP

The total for each of these column ranges is calculated in the corresponding subtotal cell. In our example, we must calculate the subtotal to be entered in cell D10.

> You have to enter an equal sign at the beginning of the formula to activate the formula bar and tell Excel you're entering a formula.

Although the Sum function is easiest to use, the following method is more flexible:

1. Enter the following formula in this cell:

   `=sum()`

2. In the formula bar, click between the two parentheses. The cursor will blink here in confirmation.

QUICK TIP

> Insert the range reference for the expenditure amounts. Although this example range is small, and you could just enter the reference as "D3:D9", we want you to get some practice. While the formula bar is active, your mouse pointer is also a cell pointer. When you click a cell, its reference is inserted where the cursor is located in the formula bar.

5   Creating Worksheets

CAUTION!

3. Position your mouse pointer on cell D3, then drag the pointer to D9. Release the mouse button and the range reference is automatically entered in the formula bar.

> You can move the selection border back and forth when selecting ranges, as long as you hold down the mouse button. If you release the button, you end that selection.

You'll probably use the Sum function for subtotals in future worksheets. However, this method is convenient when you need to enter references within a function's parentheses. It also prevents any typing errors. Remember to confirm the formula in your formula bar by clicking the green checkmark or by pressing Enter.

How does a formula work? It processes numbers, called "constants", and cell or range references using math operators (+,-,*,/, and ^). The formula's result can change if the cell or range to which it refers changes its value.

↓ X ✗	=sum(D3:D9)	
B	**C**	**D**
		January
		0.00
		0.00
		0.00
		0.00
		0.00
		0.00
		0.00
	Subtotal	=sum(D3:D9)

For more information on the Sum function, see Chapter 4.

Copying and moving formulas

Pointing references   You can enter more than just numbers and text in an Excel cell. Dates and times, as well as formulas can be entered. When you enter a formula in a cell, the result of the formula's calculation is displayed in that cell. However, the formula bar continues to display the formula.

Like other cell contents, formulas can be copied and moved. You can use the same method to copy, fill and move cells containing formulas as you use with other cells. Let's practice doing this.

The first formula we entered is in cell D10. Copy this formula (the cell contents) to cells E10 through O10, using one of the methods we described. We recommend you do the following:

1. Move to D10 and position your mouse pointer on the selection border's fill handle.

2. Drag the fill handle to cell O10.

3. When you reach the right edge of the window, the visible portion of the worksheet shifts to show the newly selected cells. Now you can see when you reach cell O10.

4. Release the mouse button and the formula from D10 is pasted in all the cells you just moved across.

Relative and absolute references

Look closely at the formula bar when you select cell E10 now. Excel didn't just copy the contents of D10 - =SUM(D3:D9). It adjusted this formula to fit each column reference. This intelligent copy function makes it very easy to fill cells with certain formulas.

This form of referencing, in which Excel changes the column reference to suit the new cell, is called relative referencing. You can transform an absolute reference to a relative one.

Excel can also copy formulas using what's called absolute referencing. When you copy or move formulas with absolute referencing, the references don't change. Some formulas refer to the same reference, regardless of the formula's location. Specify the references in the formula as absolute before you copy or move the formula, by first bringing the formula into the formula bar. Place the text cursor between the absolute reference's column and row coordinates. Press F4 and two dollar signs are entered in the reference. These indicate that the entire reference is now absolute.

To make an absolute reference relative, bring the formula into the formula bar again. Place the cursor between the reference's coordinates, and press F4. One of the dollar signs disappears. Now press F4 again, and the remaining dollar sign moves in front of the column coordinate. Press F4 one more time and this dollar sign disappears, turning the reference into a relative one.

Finish entering Sum functions in the remaining subtotal cells. Enter each formula in column D with the correct reference, then copy this formula to the remaining cells in the row:

Creating Worksheets

- Move to cell A3 and insert a row of cells. Select **Rows** from the **Insert** menu. A row of blank cells is inserted.

- Enter "Income" in cell A3. Select cell D3. Type "0". Fill cells E3 through O3 with zeros as described. Don't forget to specify the number format for the cells.

- Insert enough rows below the first income row to accommodate all your sources of income. After you insert the first row of cells, select **Repeat Insert Rows** from the **Edit** menu. Then select cells D3 through O3 and copy the contents of the new cells.

- Enter "Total Income" in cell A6. Cell D6 is the subtotal of cells D3 through D5. Place the formula (=SUM(D3:D5)) in D6, then copy this formula to cells E6 through O6.

You now have the subtotals for the individual groups, but not for the expenditure and income categories. Insert a blank row after the last income row using **Rows** from the **Insert** menu. Enter "Total Expenditures" as a title in the first column of the row.

Do this for the income now. These rows are blank, so you don't need to do any inserting. If you have filled more rows than you need with zeros, delete the extra rows now. In this example, delete the range from row 34 to 50. Select rows 34 to 50 and press ⒟ⒺⓁ. You just removed all the extra zeros.

Cell A7 now reads "Total Expenditures". Below this, insert a new row named "Balance". Now we need the corresponding formulas. Move to column D in the row that's assigned to the sum of expenditures (cell D28 in our example). In this cell, the sum of the fixed and flexible expenditures will be calculated. This can be done with a simple formula:

1. Enter an equal sign (=).

2. Click D17 with your mouse pointer. This cell contains the subtotal of the expenditures. Therefore, the reference D17 is entered in the formula bar just after the equal sign. Type a plus sign.

3. Click your mouse pointer on cell D27 (containing the subtotal of flexible expenditures). This reference is inserted after the plus sign in the formula bar.

4. Complete the entry by pressing [Enter].

You can also copy this formula across the worksheet. Use this as the model for the income Sum function.

Cells D7 through O7 are total expenditures. This is a repeat of the information in cells D28 through O28.

Select cell D7 and enter an equal sign in the formula bar. Scroll the screen and select cell D28, the subtotal of expenditures, and press [Enter].

The value from field D28 is copied into cell D7. Copy cell D7 to cells E7 through O7.

This is a good time to add a few touches to your worksheet, such as bold type, etc. Make those changes now.

Your finished worksheet should look something like this:

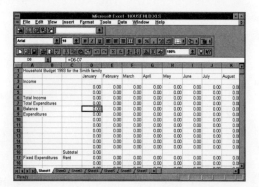

The formula for the balance is very similar except that, instead of adding two references, this formula subtracts one from the other. Try it yourself. For our example worksheet, you should get =D6-D7 in cell D8.

5 | Creating Worksheets

Range Names

You may have some trouble working with ranges in complex worksheets, due to the strange combinations of numbers, letters, and colons. Excel lets you assign names to these ranges so you can reference them more easily. Choose names that are more or less self-explanatory.

Practice using range names in the Household Budget worksheet. Later, you'll use these names in the Sum functions. This is how you might name the range containing the fixed expenditures for the month of January:

1. Select the range with the fixed expenditures for January (D18 to D26 in the sample worksheet).

2. Select **Name/Define...** in the **Insert** menu, which opens a dialog box. Under "Refers to:", look for the selected range's reference. For this example, enter the following name in the "Name" field:

```
January_fixed_expenditures [Enter]
```

3. Click [OK] to confirm the name. The following figure illustrates this exercise: Now the range $D$18:$D$26 in Sheet1 is called "January_fixed_expenditures".

Now the range $D$18:$D$26 in Sheet1 is called "January_fixed_expenditures". Let's try another exercise. Delete cell D27, where January's fixed expenditures are subtotaled. Select D27 again, enter an equal sign to activate the formula bar, then enter the SUM() function:

```
=sum()
```

Place your text cursor between the parentheses. Select **Name/Paste...** from the **Insert** menu. A dialog box opens, displaying all the range names. It only includes the one you just defined. Select this name and click [OK]. Excel inserts this range in the formula's parentheses, by its name. Press [Enter] to confirm your entry. Now cell D27 contains the following formula:

```
=SUM(January_fixed_expenditures)
```

Placing real values in the cells

You can now enter the amounts in cells D18 to D26. Remember, you don't need to enter digits beyond the decimal point if the number is whole. Based on your number format selection, Excel automatically adds trailing zeros where necessary. Whenever you type and confirm an entry, Excel updates the subtotal in D27.

The Define Name dialog box

When you're done with that exercise, enter names for the fixed expenditure ranges for the remaining months. Then name the flexible expenditure, fixed income, and flexible income ranges for all the months.

Range names in formulas

Use these range names in your formulas to make them more understandable to you and other users. For instance, move to cell D28 and replace its contents with:

```
=Sum(January_fixed_expenditures)+Sum(January_flexible_expenditures)
```

Don't forget to press Enter to confirm this new formula. This produces the following result:

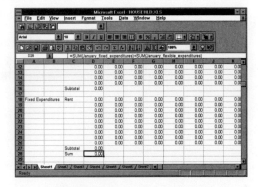

Household Budget worksheet with amounts

5 | Creating Worksheets

Let's say you want to use the column after December for the annual subtotal for each item. It would be helpful to name the range of the twelve cells in each row. Try this for the rent/mortgage amounts (row 18 in our example):

1. Select the cells, including the title cell, from B18 to O18.

2. Select **Name/Create...** from the **Insert** menu. In the dialog box which opens, notice the option "Left column" is checked. This indicates that this range's name will be taken from the first column on the left.

3. Click [OK]. Now the title of the row is also the range name for this subtotal.

You can even use this method to assign several range names at the same time:

1. Select the range of cell B18 to cell O26, all fixed expenditures.

2. Select **Name/Define...** from the **Insert** menu.

3. Don't change anything in the following dialog box, just click [OK].

Each row range now has the same name as the row's title. And you did it all in just one operation.

Functions

A function is a type of automatic calculation, assembled from basic math operators. Functions simplify formulas. Excel offers 180 functions and lets you create your own. The SUM() function, for example, makes addition a lot more simple. The following formula

```
=D3+D4+D5+D6+D7+D8+D9
```

can be simplified with the SUM() function:

```
=SUM(D3:D9)
```

You always have to begin a formula with an equal sign. Then enter the function's name precisely or Excel will treat the entry as text.

Arguments

The two parentheses at the end of every function contain the function's argument. An argument is the set of values or cells on which you want the function to act. Excel offers different ways to simplify the use of functions.

Insert a function

Practice implementing a function in the Household Budget worksheet. Calculate how much money you spend on gasoline in cell P12. Select cells D12 through O12 and click **Name/Define...** in the **Insert** menu. In the dialog box that opens, click OK. You now have a range named "Gasoline".

Row 12 displays your monthly gasoline expenditures. Enter an amount for each month in these cells. Add these figures in cell P12. Enter the following in this cell:

```
=sum(gasoline)
```

Don't forget to press Enter.

The method we just discussed is called the manual method. The following is called the semi-automatic method:

1. Move to cell Q12.

2. Select **Function...** from the **Insert** menu, opening a dialog box similar to the number format dialog box. The left list box shows the different categories (such as "Math & Trig"), and the right list box displays the functions available for this category.

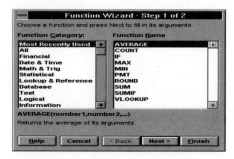

The first Function Wizard dialog box

3. Select the "Statistical" category.

4. Choose "AVERAGE" from the list of corresponding functions.

5. Close the dialog box with (Finish).

Your formula bar now contains:

```
=AVERAGE(number1,number2,...)
```

The number1 parameter is selected. Type the range reference for gasoline expenditures now. Instead of typing it in, Excel offers another way. Put the cursor between the parentheses and select all text between the parentheses. Select **Name/Paste...** from the **Insert** menu. Select the range name you need (gasoline, for our example), and click (OK). Now your formula bar should contain:

```
=AVERAGE(Gasoline)
```

Press (Enter) to confirm this function. The average of the monthly gasoline expenditures for the year immediately appears in cell Q12.

All the functions

Choose **Function...** from the **Insert** menu. Select the "All" category in the "Function Category:" list box. The corresponding function list is long and confusing. However, you sometimes need to select this category, for instance when you don't know where a function is filed.

To avoid scrolling through the list of 180 functions, click the top entry in the "Function Wizard - 1 of 2" dialog box, then type the first letter of the function you want. If you're looking for the MAX() function, press M. The list automatically scrolls to the first name that starts with "M". Just scroll through this part of the list to find "MAX()".

Chapter 12 contains a list of the most important functions, as well as some application examples. This chapter also examines the meanings of the different function arguments.

Possible Problems Creating Worksheets

Obviously, you use different methods to create large and complex worksheets in Excel. This section lists possible errors and their solutions.

I'm getting disoriented in my worksheet

When you create a large worksheet, you have to plan it out before you actually produce it. Make a written list of what you want to accomplish with the worksheet. Then sketch the worksheet's layout on paper. Consider what you need to enter in the cells, and what you'll calculate. Then start Excel.

QUICK TIP

If you started a complicated worksheet without properly planning it, you may very well be lost now. Abort your project and start over. Go back to the planning stage. Most likely, it will take less time to produce your worksheet if you start over, than if you try to correct the problems.

When I save my worksheet, Excel asks whether it should replace something

Excel keeps an eye on what you save. When you save a new worksheet, you usually assign your own name to the worksheet file. If you choose a name belonging to another file in this directory, Excel displays the following warning:

File replacement warning

A directory can't contain two worksheets with the same file name. If you answer this warning message with OK, Excel replaces the worksheet that is presently stored in the directory with the one you're saving. So, the original worksheet no longer exists. If you answer with Cancel, Excel asks you for a different file name. We recommend that you do this when you aren't sure whether to replace the existing file.

The numbers in the cells look wrong

The way a number looks in a cell may be different from the way you entered the number in the formula bar. Excel displays your entry according to the number format you had selected. Number format determines, among other things, how many decimal places will be displayed. If you enter a number with more digits beyond the decimal point than the number format will accept, Excel rounds that entry.

Check the number format you selected and change it if necessary. Move to the cell with the value and click **Number** in the **Format** menu. Look in the right list box or in the lower-left text box to see what you chose. "Sample" displays the selected cell in your chosen number format. Determine exactly how you want the number to be formatted, then click OK.

I copied a cell, but I can only paste it once

You can only copy a cell's contents to the Clipboard if you select **Copy**, then **Paste** at least once (both in the **Edit** menu). If you use the quick method to copy, you can only copy once. To copy the contents of a cell repeatedly, do the following:

1. Go to the cell you want to copy.

2. Select **Copy** from the **Edit** menu. Look for the marquee type of border around the cell.

3. Go to the first target cell and select **Paste** from the **Edit** menu.

4. Go to the next target cell and select **Paste** from the **Edit** menu again.

5. Continue this until you've copied the contents into every target cell.

I accidentally edited the wrong cells when I was filling a range of cells

Say you want to fill several cells with the contents of one cell. One of the cells you fill already had information in it. If you use the AutoFill feature, dragging the starting cell's border fill handle over the cells, Excel simply overwrites this information. To retrieve the information, you need to undo the AutoFill feature. Select **Edit Undo: AutoFill**.

You can only retrieve the information this way if you haven't done anything else in Excel since you used AutoFill. If this command appears in grey type (meaning it can't be selected) or if it doesn't say **Undo: AutoFill**, you can no longer restore the information in that cell.

I can't move a cell

You can easily miss and select another cell instead of the border of the cell you want. Be careful to gently press the mouse button when the mouse pointer is turning into an arrow. Perhaps the following method will work for you:

1. Select the cell you want to move.

2. Select **Cut** from the **Edit** menu.

3. Move your mouse pointer to the target location.

4. Press Enter and Excel cuts the cell from its original location and pastes it in the new place.

Creating Worksheets

When I insert a row, I get a weird dialog box

You want to insert a new row, so you click **Cells...** from the **Insert** menu. You figure Excel will insert a new row now; instead, the "Insert" dialog box appears. This opens when you try to insert cells that don't form a complete row or column. Simply click "Entire Row", then (OK), and a blank row is inserted above the selected one.

Insert Cells dialog box

Excel only inserts an empty row if you select an entire row, then click the command. Click the row coordinate button and a new row is inserted above the selected one. The same goes for inserting columns.

My formula doesn't work

If you enter a formula in the formula bar, then confirm it, you expect to see the result in the active cell. Instead, the cell displays the formula. There are several reasons why this may happen:

1. Excel is incorrectly configured on your system. Select **Options...** from the **Tools** menu. If you see a little X in the "Formulas" list box, Excel is configured to display formulas instead of results. Click this check box to remove the X, then close the dialog box by clicking (OK).

2. You forgot to include the equal sign in the formula. Excel only recognizes a formula if it begins with an equal sign. Select the cell and click the formula bar directly in front of the first letter. When you see a blinking text cursor here, enter the equal sign. Click the green checkmark to close the formula bar.

3. You made a typographical error when you entered the formula. Excel can only understand functions that are typed correctly. If you enter Sums() instead of Sum(), Excel reads this as a piece of text. You also have to enter cell references correctly. If you enter a space between the column and row coordinates, for instance, Excel won't recognize it as a cell reference. Excel is also very picky about how you enter numbers.

Remember not to use spaces in formulas or functions. You can call a column or row "My worksheet", but you can't call a range reference this because of the space in the phrase.

QUICK TIP

> Whenever you can, use your mouse pointer to show Excel what you mean, especially with function arguments. Enter a cell or range reference within a formula or function by pointing to the cell or range with your mouse pointer. Excel then inserts (without typos) the coordinates of the selected cell or range. Another typo saver is to enter an equal sign then select **Function...** from the **Insert** menu. Click the name of the function you want in the dialog box that opens, then close the dialog box.

I copied a formula, but it produced the wrong result

Excel automatically modifies the formula's references to suit the new location when it copies formulas. Say cell A4 contains the following formula:

    =SUM(A1:A3)

When you copy this to cell C23, Excel interprets the formula for the new location, and it now reads:

    =SUM(C19:C22)

If you don't want Excel to change the formula's references when it copies it, switch the formula to absolute referencing. Select the cell containing the formula and click the formula bar. Set the text cursor between the letter and the number of a reference, then press F4. Then our example reads:

    =SUM($A$1:A3)

But we're still not done. Click the text cursor between the column and row coordinates of the second reference and press F4 again. The formula now reads:

    =SUM($A$1:$A$3)

The dollar sign indicates that the reference is absolute; it cannot be changed when the cell is copied or moved. Copy the formula to cell C23 and notice that it didn't change at all:

```
=SUM($A$1:$A$3)
```

TAKE NOTE

> References are normally relative and have no dollar signs when they appear in the formula bar. When you need absolute references, you have to manually change them. If you want to change absolute references to relative ones, you also have to do this manually. Select the cell and click the formula bar, then set the text cursor between the reference's letter and number. Press F4 three times successively and you'll see a different combination each time; the third time's the charm.

For example, "$A$1", after the first time you press F4, becomes "$A1". The second time you press F4, the reference becomes "A$1". When you press F4 the third time, the reference becomes A1.

I don't know how to use a range name

What good is the most wonderful range name you select if you need to memorize it in order to use it? Of course, it's easier than that to use range names in your formulas. Select the cell containing the formula in which you want to insert the name, and select **Name/Define...** from the **Insert** menu. Click the desired range name in the list box and close the dialog box. Excel then inserts the name.

I can't find the function I need

With 180 functions, it's easy to lose track of the one you need. Excel's dialog box, under **Function...** from the **Insert** menu, can help. Select the category where you think the function is located in the left-hand list box. Then look for the function in the list on the right.

Chapter 6

Impressive Charts

If you have a worksheet that completely fits into the space on your screen, you can probably work with it more easily. This is logical to assume, since you avoid a lot of scrolling. However, it's almost impossible to produce this type of worksheet, since you usually have a lot more information to depict. The worksheet gets larger as the amount of information increases.

One way to solve this problem is to use Excel charts. Although we will use it, our Household Budget worksheet doesn't make a good example. The following are more realistic applications for Excel charts:

- A graph of the sales levels of different branches throughout the year.

- A curve diagram describing different depreciation projections over time.

- A pie chart displaying aspects of a product's total cost.

- A bar chart of vote counts following an election.

This chapter shows you how to create charts from the worksheet numbers. It also discusses types of charts: Area, bar, line, pie, and special types. You learn how to label a chart. And you also deal with the aesthetic qualities of appearance and color. Finally, this chapter discusses possible errors in chart creation.

Impressive Charts

Creating Charts from Worksheet Information

To help you create a chart, Excel offers a small utility program, called the ChartWizard. This uses a series of dialog boxes to lead you through the process of setting up a chart.

Before you work with the ChartWizard, you need to select the cells you want the chart to represent. In our example, select the range of monthly balances. Move to the range's first cell, press the left mouse button, and drag the selection to the end of the range. Release the mouse button, and the cells are inverse (white font on a black background), as shown below:

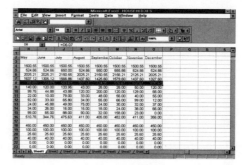

Selected cells

Now start the ChartWizard. Click the ChartWizard toolbar button. It looks like it's pressed down when it's selected:

When you move your mouse pointer back to the worksheet, notice how its appearance changes. It now looks like a fine set of crosshairs. Use this pointer to select an area of your worksheet that will later contain your chart. You should try to define the area next to or below any occupied cells.

CAUTION!

Excel always places charts directly on the worksheet, even if the chart is a separate file. You can place the chart anywhere, including over filled cells. Of course, it's difficult to access the covered cell's information, so don't cover any cells you need to access.

In our Household Budget worksheet, place the chart below the filled cells. Scroll down until the bottom row appears at the upper edge of the window and column A appears at the left edge. Scroll across to reach the right edge of filled cells. Move your mouse pointer back onto the worksheet so it looks like a set of crosshairs again.

Now define the chart area. You can draw it anywhere, not just along the cell division lines. Later you can change its size and position. For this exercise, position your mouse pointer on cell B30, then drag the mouse button to cell G45. Release the mouse pointer only after you made the rectangular area the desired shape and size.

> This rectangle may look small now, but the chart will be completely visible later.

QUICK TIP

The ChartWizard dialog boxes

When you release the mouse button, the first ChartWizard dialog box opens. Notice that the title bar tells you it's the first of five ChartWizard dialog boxes.

All these dialog boxes contain the same buttons. Abort the chart creation with [Cancel]. Go to the next dialog box with [Next>]. Go to the preceding dialog box and make any changes with [<Back]. Go to the first dialog box and enter a different range with [|<<]. Avoid clicking [>>], since it jumps over all the subsequent steps of the ChartWizard and doesn't let you confirm their information or make adjustments.

ChartWizard 1 defines the range

Impressive Charts

The range you defined is listed under "Range". We'll accept this range for this exercise. However, Excel lets you change the range now if you wish. Either enter different coordinates (something we don't recommend) or use the mouse pointer to choose another range. Click (Next>) to accept the range.

The second dialog box lets you choose the type of chart to create. Can you recognize the different charts from these little illustrations? The second section of this chapter discusses the different types of charts.

Chart Wizard 2 defines the type of chart

Click the picture of the type of chart you want to create, and the selection is displayed inverse. Select the column bar chart for our example. Then click (Next>) to move to the next dialog box.

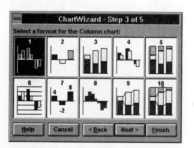

Chart Wizard 3 defines the type of format

The third dialog box is a little complicated. For each chart type, Excel offers 10 chart formats, most pertaining to the arrangement of chart components. For instance, select Format 2 for your vertical bar chart, to widen the bars. Click the appropriate picture, then click [Next>] to move to the next dialog box.

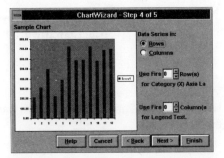

Chart Wizard 4 determines how things are converted

This dialog box shows how your chart is shaping up. If you want to change its appearance, return to the appropriate dialog box and make the change. Otherwise, skip over this dialog box by clicking [Next>].

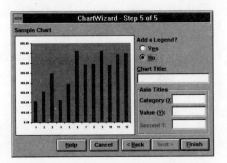

Chart Wizard 5 defines the chart labels

The fifth dialog box contains four text boxes. These define labels for the chart to effectively represent the chart's individual components. Each of the vertical bars in our chart represents a monthly balance.

Impressive Charts

Excel arranges charts within a coordinate system. A two-dimensional chart has an X and a Y axis. The X axis refers to the different categories and the Y axis displays each category's size. A three-dimensional chart includes a Z axis, which orders the different rows.

The chart's title is self-explanatory. Click "Chart Title" and enter:

```
Monthly Balances
```

Within a couple seconds, the title is displayed in the little sample chart. Label the X axis and the individual bars now. Click "Category (X)" and enter:

```
Months
```

Then click "Value (Y)" and type:

```
Amount in Dollars
```

All these labels are displayed in the miniature chart. It isn't as easy to enter the month names by the individual bars (or in the form of a legend). You'll learn about this later in the chapter.

Instead of a Next> button, this dialog box has a Finish button. Click this to end the ChartWizard. Your chart should now appear on your worksheet.

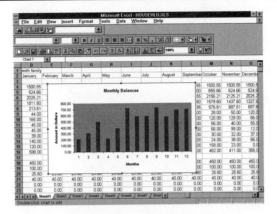

The chart on the worksheet

Changing the location and size of the chart

Now that you can see the chart in the worksheet, you can determine whether you need to change anything. You can even move the chart. Practice moving your chart now. Position your mouse pointer on the chart, press and hold your mouse button, then drag the chart to another location. Release the mouse button when you get to the new location.

The chart is now selected but, unlike cells and ranges, it doesn't appear inverse. Instead, a thin border with eight small square selection squares surrounds it. Use these selection squares to change the chart's size, enlarging or reducing it. Move one of the four squares at the four corners of the border to change the size in a specific direction. For example, drag the lower-right selection square down and to the right to enlarge the chart.

> Another indication that the chart is selected is the additional toolbar at the lower edge of your screen.

TAKE NOTE

Move the upper-left selection square to the lower right to reduce the chart. You can only move the selection squares on the sides horizontally or vertically.

Now practice moving and resizing your chart in the worksheet:

1. Click the chart to select it.

2. Press and hold the mouse button.

3. Drag the chart to the lower-left and release the mouse button when the chart's upper-right corner is at about cell A38.

4. Choose the selection square at the bottom of the chart border and notice that the mouse pointer turns into a vertical double arrow.

5. Press and hold the mouse button, then drag the border upward until the chart's lower edge lies somewhere in row 44. The chart is modified to fit within the space available. Of course, at some sizes, you can't even read the chart.

6. Now choose the selection square at the lower-right corner and notice that the mouse pointer turns into a diagonal double arrow.

7. Drag the selection square until it reaches approximately cell F52, then release the mouse button.

Saving the chart

Now that the workbook is updated, this is probably a good time to save it on your hard drive. Select **Save** from the **File** menu. Excel automatically saves the updated version of the workbook under the name that appears in the title bar.

Types of Charts

There are different types of charts for the different types of information you want to represent. This section introduces the Excel chart types and explains their characteristics. Each is pictured for your reference as well.

Area charts

An area chart represents values as continuous lines, and fills the surfaces between these lines with color. This chart type is useful when you want to compare a lot of values and their sums. The following area chart example deals with measurement data:

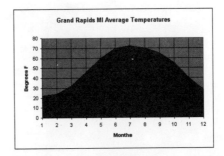

Area chart

Your area chart can even look three-dimensional:

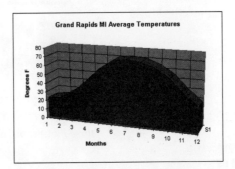

A three-dimensional area chart

Bar charts and column charts

Use bar charts and column charts when you have to compare only a small number of values or categories. These charts display the categories as bars, horizontally or vertically, of differing lengths in comparison to one another.

Impressive Charts

The bar chart can effectively compare three or four categories. The column chart, on the other hand, can compare up to a dozen categories. If you need to compare more than a dozen categories or values, a surface or line chart will work better.

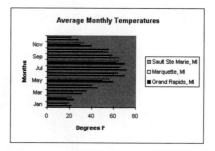

Bar chart

Again, you can give either of these chart types the appearance of three dimensions:

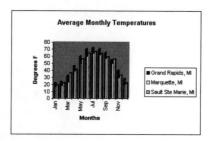

A three-dimensional column chart

Line charts

A line chart is basically an area chart without the areas. It displays values as continuous lines. Use a line chart when comparing positive and negative values or changes in magnitude. Line charts handle large quantities of values easily. The following example is a modified measurement value chart:

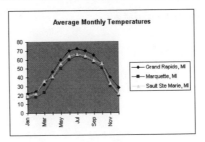

Line chart

You can also use an intersecting format option in line charts. Select a logarithmic magnitude axis and Excel will automatically and accurately place the data points on this scale. It can even generate maximum, minimum, and average representations automatically.

Pie charts

Use pie charts to show how parts of the whole are distributed. Values are represented as different sizes of pie slices. Pie charts restrict you to displaying only one row or column of values. Remember this when you start the ChartWizard.

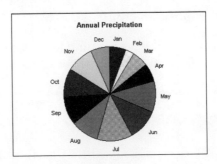

Pie chart

You can make another effective comparison by displaying comparable rows or columns in side-by-side pie charts.

6 | Impressive Charts

Special types of charts

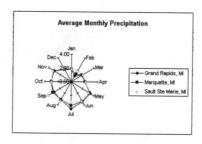

Radar charts

In a Radar chart, each set receives its own axis. These axes all intersect at a common centerpoint. Use this type of chart for scientific calculations and other special representations.

3-D Surface charts

With 3-D surface charts, you can graphically represent massive amounts of information in three dimensions. You usually see this sort of chart illustrating the results of differential and integral calculations.

Combination/Overlapping charts

You can combine bars and lines in combination, or overlapping charts. Use this sort of chart to display stock diagrams, for instance.

Labeling Your Chart

When you worked with the ChartWizard, you entered a chart title as well as titles for the axes. To label individual elements like the vertical bars, you start the chart creation a little differently.

Select not only the cells containing the values to be represented, but also the cells containing the names for these values. Delete your old chart before practicing this with the Household Budget worksheet.

Simply click the chart to select it. A frame with selection squares surrounds it. Press Backspace and Excel deletes the chart, without asking for confirmation.

> If you delete a chart by accident, select **Edit Undo Clear** right away.

The labeling process

First select the two ranges to display in your new chart:

1. Shift the visible portion of your worksheet until you can see the row containing the names of the twelve months.

2. Select these cells, D2 through O2. Press Shift + F8 to turn on Add mode.

3. Shift the visible portion of the worksheet until you can see the row containing the monthly balances, row 8.

4. Press 8 to turn on Extend mode.

5. Select cells D8 through O8.

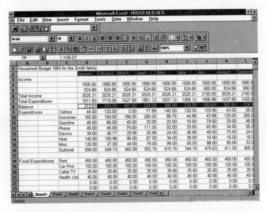

Two non-contiguous ranges of cells are selected

6 | Impressive Charts

Both ranges should be selected. Click the ChartWizard toolbar button. Mark an area for the chart. Then the first ChartWizard dialog box will open and you'll see the following reference values in the text box:

```
=$D$2:$O$2,$D$8:$O$8
```

Notice the comma in the formula. It indicates the ChartWizard now uses both of the ranges you selected. Follow the ChartWizard steps. When you're done, the month names will be included as the bar labels.

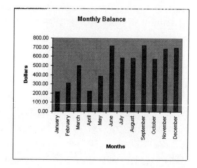

The bars in this example are labeled

Adding labels

Excel manages certain labels in a special way and refers to these as "assigned text". Double-click the chart. Choose the **Titles...** command in your **Insert** menu. A dialog box opens in which you specify which label object to add.

Titles dialog box

The dialog box identifies the X axis as "Category (X) Axis". Assign a label to it:

1. Select **Titles...** from the **Insert** menu.

2. Click the "Category (X) Axis" check box in the dialog box.

3. Close the dialog box. Look closely to see a new text object just below the chart, containing just the letter X. The formula bar displays the object's name ("Text Axis 2") and contents ("X").

Now, when you click the formula bar to activate it, you can change "X" to something more informative: "Months". Always confirm your change by pressing Enter.

> You cannot move or resize these types of fixed text objects. Excel places them somewhere specific on the chart, and only moves them if you change the chart's size, shape, or position.

QUICK TIP You can assign labels to the axes and the objects representing the different values, and a title to the entire chart. It's is difficult to assign labels to the chart objects.

> Excel uses the term, data set, meaning a block of values shown in relation to one another. In our chart, the values for the monthly balances are, collectively, a data set. Each value in the set results in what Excel terms a data point.

NERD TALK If you only want to label a single vertical bar, select **Data Labels...** from the **Insert** menu. Click the "Show Label" option button to state the label, or click "Show Value" to specify the value. Close the box by clicking OK, and the label appears on the bar. The label's contents are identical to the value on the bar.

Deleting labels

Delete labels the same way you delete cell contents. Move to the label and press Backspace. This activates the empty formula bar. Press Enter to confirm your deletion.

6 | Impressive Charts

Edit the chart directly, as we'll discuss in the next section, to delete more quickly. Select the label and simply press Del. The object is deleted right away. Use this method to delete the labels for the X axis ("Months") and the Y axis ("Dollars") if they're on your chart.

QUICK TIP   Chapter 10 has detailed information on labeling charts.

Dressing Up Your Chart

To make cosmetic changes to your chart, double-click the chart to edit it. This provides you with almost unlimited possibilities for changes. Remember, you want the chart and the entire worksheet to be easy to read and comprehend.

Direct chart editing can become addictive. You might find yourself experimenting with all these possibilities so much that you forget your objective. Keep the chart effective and understandable.

WARNING!

Editing a chart

To switch to chart editing, select the chart then double-click it. Two things confirm you are in chart edit mode:

1. The menu bar shows fewer and different names.

2. The chart border changes.

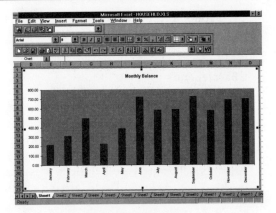

Chart editing mode

This type of chart consists of a series of objects, and each of these has a specific name. It's easy to find out the name of each object. Click the object or a portion of the chart that you think is an object, then look in the formula bar. The object's name appears at one end of the bar and, at the other end, the object's contents.

Click your chart's title, "Monthly Balance". Eight white selection squares surround the field in which this word is located. The formula bar displays the object's name, "Title".

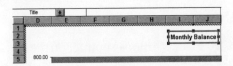

The edit mode formula bar

Let's change our chart's title:

1. Click the title, "Monthly Balance"; white selection squares mark the field.

2. Select the text, "Monthly Balance".

3. Delete the existing text by pressing Backspace.

109

4. Type "Plus and Minus".

5. Press (Enter) to confirm the change.

Chart legends

The chart legend identifies which color represents which category. Our example chart doesn't use different colors, so we can't apply this function. If your chart compares several categories, select **Legend** from the **Insert** menu. Excel automatically creates the legend and places it in the chart. After it's just been created, the legend is selected. If you wish, move it now by dragging the legend's surface with your mouse pointer.

To delete a legend, you have to select it first. Click the legend, and a frame with selection squares surrounds it. Press (Del) now.

Chart arrows

You can add an arrow to your chart to accent a particular element like a monthly balance. Select **Toolbars...** from the **View** menu. Activate the "Drawing" check box and click (OK). Click the arrow toolbar button and draw the arrow.

To drag the entire arrow, grab the arrow shaft with your mouse pointer, something like this:

1. Click the arrow.

2. Place the mouse pointer on the black selection square at the tip of the arrow.

3. Press and hold the mouse button, then drag the selection square to the new location.

4. Release the mouse button.

Delete the arrow by first selecting it. Click its shaft and the selection squares appear again. Then press (Del).

There is no limit, except aesthetics, to the number of arrows you can include in your chart. However, you can't add an arrow if one is currently selected. To remove the selection from the arrow, simply click the mouse pointer elsewhere on the chart.

Attaching text

An arrow by itself doesn't say much. Place some text where the arrow starts to explain why it's pointing to a particular object. You can add these text objects very easily:

1. Make sure no other text objects, such as titles, axes, or labels, are selected. If any are, click the mouse pointer elsewhere on the chart to unselect them.

2. Click the empty formula bar to activate it.

3. Enter the text, for instance, "July is the warmest month in Grand Rapids", then press Enter.

The new text object appears in the middle of the chart. Eight selection squares surround this selection. While you drag it to the new location, notice that the object is just a border; the text remains in the original location. When you release the mouse button at the new location, the text jumps into the border again.

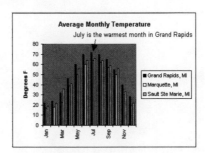

Chart with text and arrow

Delete these types of text objects in the usual way: Select the object, then press Del.

Impressive Charts

Changing colors

Always remember when you want to change one of an object's properties, you have to select the object first. Click all the different components of the chart now. Notice that the official name of the selected element is displayed on the left side of the formula bar.

If you click one of the red vertical bars in your chart, you'll see "S1" displayed in the left half of the formula bar. This indicates that you clicked one of the objects belonging to the series number 1. The right part of the formula bar displays a complicated formula. This shows which worksheet data are transformed into the chart's vertical bars.

If you want to change the color of the vertical bars, click one of the columns. Now there's a letter and number in the formula bar referring to the series number. Select **Data Series...** in the **Format** menu. Click the "Patterns" tab to display the following:

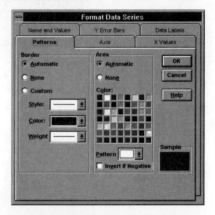

Format Data Series dialog box

The box's center group is labeled "Area" and below this are three buttons. The "Automatic" option button is probably selected, indicating that Excel will automatically pick the color for the chart's bars. If you click "None", then confirm it with OK, the bars become transparent. To pick your own color, click one of the color buttons.

Add a pattern to the chart

Click the arrow button at the right of the "Pattern" box to access a list of fill patterns. Each of these is a combination of two colors, the foreground color and background color. To create red cross-hatching on a yellow background, specify yellow as the background color and red for the foreground. Then select the desired cross-hatching or pattern.

The top line in this list, "solid color", indicates that the selected element will be filled with the foreground color. Select this entry by clicking it with your mouse pointer. This also closes the list.

If you want to return to the original color, select the object again and choose **Selected Data Series...** from the **Format** menu. In the open dialog box, click the "Automatic" button in the "Area" group. Then close the dialog box.

QUICK TIP

> Use this method to change colors throughout Excel. Change the colors of chart components as well as worksheet items. You can even set the color of the cell background.

Chapter 8 discusses this topic in detail.

Returning to your worksheet

Click on the sheet to exit this editing mode. Excel updates values in the worksheet that correspond to values you changed in the chart.

Problems Creating Charts

You can't really make any serious mistakes during chart creation. You can always delete a chart if something doesn't work right, then start a new one. We recommend that you do this whenever you have a problem with a chart. It normally takes less time than fixing the chart's problem.

Also be sure to remember that it's very easy to become trapped in a chart, trying to make it more and more beautiful. You will normally not have this kind of free time. Be more concerned about the chart's clarity and how well it represents information.

I forgot to select a range before starting the ChartWizard

The ChartWizard's first dialog box contains the reference of the most recently selected cell. You can't create a chart based on one cell's value, but you can define the range you want the chart to represent. Leave the first ChartWizard dialog box open, and shift the worksheet window until you can see this range. Select the range and its reference will appear in the dialog box. Now you can continue using the ChartWizard.

I forgot to select the range for the names

If you realize this before you enter the ChartWizard, simply go back and select them. Select the first range, then press and hold Ctrl while selecting the second range. If you remember once you're in the ChartWizard, do the following:

1. Click the |< button in the current ChartWizard dialog box to return to the first dialog box.

2. Move the mouse pointer to the "Range" text box; notice how the pointer appears as an I-beam.

3. Click to the right of the equal sign and a text cursor appears here.

4. Scroll through the worksheet to the range of cells.

5. Select this range and the range's reference will appear in the dialog box under "Range".

6. Click Next>.

7. In the ChartWizard's fourth dialog box, select "1" in the "Use First _ Row(s) for Category(X) Axis Labels" line.

8. Click OK.

I can't see my worksheet anymore

If the area you defined for your chart covers occupied cells by mistake, the chart hides these cells. Select your chart by clicking its surface. Eight selection squares now surround it. Move it by grabbing the chart surface and drag the chart to another location. This new location can be anywhere on the worksheet.

I don't know how to make cosmetic improvements to my chart

Double-click the chart. You can edit the chart directly now. Click on your sheet to return to the workbook.

Chapter 7

Polishing Your Worksheets And Charts

If you have followed Chapters 5 and 6 to create a worksheet with an accompanying chart, your document is a "diamond in the rough" that you will learn to polish in this chapter. The document is considered rough because the titles in columns A, B and C are partially hidden, and the rows containing totals don't really stand out from the other rows.

It's easy to dress up Excel documents, since all the features of the Windows interface are at your disposal. These include a wide selection of fonts, colors and border styles for worksheet cells and their contents. This chapter covers the most important ways to improve the appearance of your Excel documents on screen and in print.

On the screen, you want a well-designed worksheet that is easy to work with. Cells that require input should be distinguishable from those that simply reflect the results of your input.

In print, your document's appearance is extremely important, because the worksheets you create are usually shared with others. In Chapter 8, we discuss printing the results of your efforts. Here we'll go over the clarity and visual appeal that help ensure readers will understand your information.

An important reminder about using color

Don't forget that the most beautiful color scheme is of little use in printed documents if you don't have a color printer. Chapter 8 explains how to produce attractive black-and-white printouts from colored worksheets.

Using Fonts

Generally, your documents will be clearer if there is some variety in your display of text and numbers (fonts, sizes, styles, etc.). You have the option of either hand-picking the fonts to be used on your charts and worksheets or letting Excel use a standard font type and size. Let's look at the available fonts and try replacing what's used in our worksheet.

NERD TALK

To understand just what a font is, think of the difference between how words look in a newspaper and on a traffic sign. One of a font's primary distinctions is the presence or absence of serifs. Serifs are the little hooks that appear at the ends of the strokes making up the letters in newspaper text, for example. Traffic signs usually display sans-serif (French for "without a serif") fonts because people can read them quickly and clearly.

Remember our rule for making changes in Excel. First select, then operate. To change an element that presently applies to all worksheet cells, select the entire worksheet first. This isn't as difficult as it sounds: Simply select the entire worksheet by clicking in the upper-left corner where the bars containing the row and column coordinates intersect.

Selecting all cells

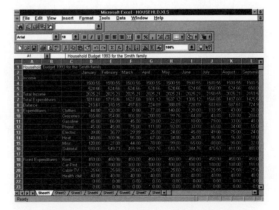

Clicking the upper left corner selects all cells

Now go to the **Format** menu (which you'll often open while you learn these exercises) and choose the **Cells...** command. Click on the "Font" tab. The rather complicated dialog box you see now allows you to make your font selection.

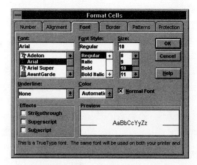

Use this dialog box to select your fonts

Other aspects of font selection

Take a look at the "Font" list box. There are several features that distinguish one font from another, from serif or sans-serif to size and boldness.

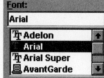

Graphic designers always seem to be coming up with new and unique styles for specialized purposes. One feature that will be very important for you will be how well it looks in print.

A list of available fonts

Printing with fonts

Running Excel under Windows, you have an added bonus, because your TrueType fonts look the same in print as they do on the screen. You know what your font, and your whole document, will look like in print, while it's still on the screen. Some printers can't print some fonts, though.

The fonts you have to choose from include those in the Windows interface as well as any you loaded onto your hard drive (from programs or when you installed the printer). Scroll through the list now and you may notice symbols next to some of the font names. These refer to how well the fonts print:

Polishing Your Worksheets And Charts

TrueType-Symbol

Fonts with this symbol are called TrueType fonts and always print well. The way they look on the screen is the way they'll look when they are printed.

Printerfont-Symbol

Fonts with this symbol are called Printer fonts and look good when printed on a particular printer. You see this symbol in your list only if the fonts that came with your printer were installed on your system.

Fonts with no symbol look best only on the screen. You may be unpleasantly surprised if you use them in printed documents.

QUICK TIP

> If you limit yourself to using only TrueType fonts, you can be sure that your documents will look good on both screen and paper. If you use fonts with the printer symbol, make sure they are for the printer that is connected to your computer.

Getting back to our exercise, select the "Arial" font, which should appear near the top of the list. This font is available on most computers. If not, just use whatever font name is currently selected.

Click the font name, then look in the large box entitled "Sample" to see what your text will look like. If it's fine, close the dialog box by clicking OK. Your worksheet text should look different, unless you were already using Arial or a very similar font.

NERD TALK

Setting font size

> Font sizes are given in units called points. This is the conventional unit of measure used in the printing trade.

The workbook's main title should be more prominent, so let's change it to a larger size. First select, then operate. Select cell A1, the cell with the workbook title ("Household Budget 1993 for the Smith Family"). Notice that the title is assigned only to this cell, although it is longer than the column is wide. Select B1 and you will see that Excel considers this cell empty, although you can see part of the title.

You'll want to remember this when you change the features of your worksheet fonts. Always be sure to select the proper cell or cells before making font changes.

Select cell A1 again and choose **Cells...** from the **Format** menu. This time, look at the "Size" list box. Here you will see a list of the available font sizes.

The numbers that appear here depend on which font is currently selected. TrueType fonts (look for the TrueType symbol) range in size from 8 to 72 points. Fonts with no symbol have small ranges of sizes. Printer fonts vary widely in their selection of sizes. For our title, select 24 point size, view it in the "Preview" box, then click OK to close the dialog box.

The title now appears on the worksheet in its new size. The row's height is adjusted to accommodate the new size.

Perhaps you also want to enlarge the row of cells with the month names. You don't have to edit the cells one at a time. Just select the range of cells (D2 to O2) containing the column headings before choosing **Cells...** from the **Format** menu. A good size here would be 12 points.

Setting font styles

The same techniques can be used to make bold or italic text. Let's make our worksheet title and the month names bold. First select the proper cells:

1. Select cell A1 (the workbook title).

2. Press Shift F8.

3. Select cells D2 to O2 (the column headings).

4. Choose **Cells...** from the **Format** menu.

5. Click "Bold" in the "Font Style" list.

6. Click [OK] to close the dialog box.

You shouldn't have any problem changing the names of the individual items in column C to italic. Try it.

Font Style:
| |
|Regular|
|Regular|
|Italic|
|Bold|
|Bold Italic|

Setting the font style

Did it work? Great. But there's an even easier way than using the **Font...** command.

Using the Toolbar

After selecting the cells containing the text you want to italicize, just click the Italic button on the toolbar - the one with the slanted "I". The text in the selected cells is immediately changed to italic.

To set bold and/or italic text back to normal, use the toolbar again. When the selected cell is bold or italic, the appropriate button looks like its pressed down. Click the button again to "release" it, and the text is restored to normal.

Use these buttons now to apply bold and italic styles to the category names (e.g., "Expenditures"). Make the headings, "Income" and "Expenditures", bold.

Aligning the text

Excel uses left alignment as the default setting for text. This means that text in a cell starts at the left edge and proceeds to the right. Numbers, on the other hand, are right-aligned. The final digit is placed at the right edge of the cell. Some of the Excel toolbar's alignment buttons determine the alignment of cell contents.

You can determine if the contents of selected cells will be right-aligned, left-aligned or centered. Centered means that the contents are placed in the cell with equal amounts of space on the left and right, assuming the text fits inside the cell.

QUICK TIP

> The "Alignment" tab from the **Format/Cells...** command gives additional alignment options. Their usefulness is normally limited to certain situations.

Chart text and fonts

The chart window also has a **Format** menu for changing fonts, but it's only available when a text element is selected. When you select it, you get a dialog box similar to the one you're already familiar with.

The options work exactly the same, except for the automatic adjustment of cell size, since a chart does not have rows and columns. When text on a chart is enlarged, it may hide other chart elements.

You can control the size and shape of the text area. If a line of text becomes too long, break it into more than one line by making the text box narrower and deeper. Just drag the lower-right handle down and to the left until the desired shape is produced. Text wrapping takes place automatically when you release the handle.

You can also use the alignment buttons on the toolbar to align chart text. The invisible borders of the text area determine the alignment.

Changing the Column Size - Width

The Household Budget worksheet already looks a lot better. There is still a serious defect, though. Some of the text doesn't show because the cells are too small. You can make them wide enough for all the text by increasing the column width. There are three ways to change column width: Manually, by specifying a value, and automatically.

Manually changing column width

You have already read about manually resizing columns in Chapter 4. Since column A needs to be widened a little, try this now.

Polishing Your Worksheets And Charts

Place the mouse pointer on the line between the column coordinates A and B at the top of the worksheet. The pointer transforms into a vertical line with right and left arrows. Drag the column border a little to the right and you'll notice that a dashed line moves with the cursor, showing how wide the column will be when you release the mouse button. At the same time, the exact width of the column is shown in the left half of the formula bar. Try to bring it precisely to 12.

What does the column width measurement actually mean? This is the average number of characters of the standard font that will fit in the column at its present width.

Specifying a value for column width

NERD TALK

To specify a certain value for the width of a column, select any cell in the column and choose **Column/Width...** from the **Format** menu.

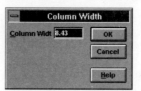

Setting the column width

Type the desired value in the "Column Width" text box. This is the active field when you open the dialog box, so it is not necessary to click it first. The number you type will replace the current value; enter 12 for our example. Then click OK to close the dialog box.

This doesn't look so great on our workbook, however. The month names have different lengths, which makes the column widths different. Uniform columns would look better, and we'll use the month with the longest name - September, in column L - as our guide.

Select this column and choose **Column Width...** again from the **Format** menu. The current width, 12.43, is displayed in the dialog box. Now proceed as follows:

1. Select columns D through O.

2. Choose **Column/Width...** from the **Format** menu.

3. Enter a column width of 12.5.

4. Click OK to close the dialog box.

All the columns are now 12.5.

If you want, you can also manually adjust the width of column A to fit text entries such as "Total Expenditures".

Changing the Row Size - Height

Although you will probably have less need for it than adjusting the width of columns, you can adjust row height as well. This feature can be put to good use for certain effects.

A larger font means a larger row height

When you increase the size of the font used in a worksheet cell, Excel automatically increases the row height to adjust to the new font size. Conversely, when you reduce the font size, the row height is automatically reduced. Try this out now on the worksheet title. Select cell B1.

Setting the row height

You can also set the row height, using the **Row/Height...** command from the **Format** menu. This command works like the one for changing column width. Simply type the desired value in the "Row Height" field. The unit of measure used here is the font's point size. Click OK to close the dialog box.

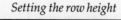

Setting the row height

If you type a row height that is too small for the font used in this row, the text will no longer be displayed properly. If this happens, open the "Row Height" dialog box again and type "12.75" (the default height). Close the dialog box by clicking OK.

WARNING!

Manually adjusting the row height

You can change row height manually much the same way you change column width. It is sometimes useful to increase a row's height to allow additional free space above the text. Drag the separator line between two adjacent row coordinates. As you drag the line, the current height is displayed in the left half of the formula bar. Use the manual method to adjust the height of line 1 to 39.00 now.

Borders Organize Worksheets

Normally when you print a worksheet, the faint lines separating the rows and columns are printed as well. They're not necessarily useful in outlining the structure of your data, however. Instead of showing the entire grid, it is often better to place borders around certain areas to help show how the data is organized. However, first you must get rid of the gridlines.

Hiding gridlines

Hide gridlines using the following steps:

1. Choose **Options...** from the **Tools** menu and click on the "View" tab. Since this command refers to the entire worksheet window, it does not matter whether any cells are selected.

2. Click the "Gridlines" check box to remove the X.

3. Click OK to close the dialog box.

Hiding a worksheet's gridlines

With the "Gridlines" check box disabled, the workbook appears with no gridlines, both on the screen and when printed. Now you can create borders that will clarify the workbook information.

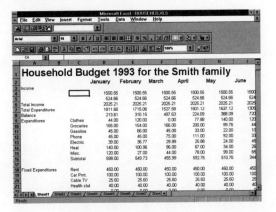

Workbook with cell gridlines removed

Making borders

Before adding borders around cells or cell ranges, don't forget to first select, then operate. This function works somewhat differently with single cells than it does with cell ranges. Try this exercise:

1. Select cell A35. This is a blank cell below the worksheet heading on our sample worksheet.

2. Choose **Cells...** from the **Format** menu and click the "Border" tab.

3. Click the rectangle next to "Outline" in the dialog box that appears, making a line segment appear inside the rectangle.

4. Click [OK] to close the dialog box.

A border now surrounds the cell. It is not obvious at first, because the selection rectangle also surrounds the cell. Move the selection rectangle away by clicking outside of cell A35. When you are done, delete cell A35.

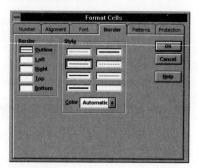

Placing a border around a cell

Making borders for a range of cells

Now let's see how borders work with a range of cells. You can use the headings of the "Fixed Expenditures" category to practice this:

1. Select the cells containing the names of the individual items (B18 through B26 in the example).

2. Choose **Cells...** from the **Format** menu and click the "Border" tab.

3. In the dialog box, click the rectangle next to "Outline". A line segment appears in the rectangle. This indicates that the entire cell range will be surrounded by a border in the selected weight.

4. Click the heaviest line from the choices in the lower area of the dialog box. This is the rightmost selection on the first line. The newly selected line weight appears in the "Outline" field.

5. Click OK to close the dialog box.

When you click outside the selected worksheet area, the new border becomes visible. The previously selected range is completely surrounded by a thick line.

Adding dividing lines

Now we would like to add dividing lines between the individual items. Select the same cell range again and choose **Cells...** from the **Format** menu. You may be dismayed by what you see: The fields in the dialog box are quite different from what we saw just a moment ago.

This is one of the pitfalls of drawing borders in Excel. You have to proceed with some caution, since it isn't always obvious what is going on. The "Left" and "Right" fields show the heavy line segment, but "Top" and "Bottom" are shaded in gray. This indicates that not all cells of the selected range have top and bottom borders.

So, how do we get a heavy line around the whole range and thin lines between the cells? First, all five rectangles must be cleared. Click those that contain a line segment to clear them. Those that are shaded in gray must be clicked twice.

Now click the "Outline" field again and the heavy line reappears. Then click "Left" and the heavy line appears here also. This is the wrong weight, however, so select a thinner line from the available border styles. As soon as you select a new style, it replaces the heavy line for the current ("Left") border position. Continue with the remaining positions until they all show the thinner line. Then close the dialog box by clicking OK.

Removing borders

To remove borders, select the desired cell or range and again choose **Cells...** from the **Format** menu. Then clear all five border positions and close the dialog box by clicking $\boxed{\text{OK}}$. If you still see borders, they belong to adjacent cells. You have to select these cells, then remove the appropriate borders.

Adding borders one at a time

You can add different borders to an individual cell at any time. Just select the cell, open the "Border" dialog box, and specify the desired styles for the border positions one at a time. First click the desired position to make it the current entry. Then click the desired style, and it will be applied to the current position. Do this for each of the cell's four sides, then click $\boxed{\text{OK}}$ to close the dialog box.

Drawing separation borders

You should use simple border designs, like a heavy line around the entire worksheet with lighter lines separating ranges of cells. We'll do this to the Household Budget worksheet now:

1. Remove all the borders you just created during the practice.

2. Select the entire worksheet (A1 through O29).

3. Choose **Cells...** from the **Format** menu and click the "Border" tab.

4. Click "Outline" in the dialog box, and select the heaviest line weight.

5. Close the dialog box with $\boxed{\text{OK}}$.

Separating titles

A heavy line should also separate the title from the rest of the worksheet. There are two ways to do this. Either add a bottom border to every cell of row 1 or a top border to every cell of row 2. Use whichever procedure you prefer, but try to be consistent throughout the worksheet.

Let's use the latter procedure in our example. Select the cells of row 2 from columns A through O. Choose **Cells...** from the **Format** menu. Click "Top" in the dialog box, and select the heavy line style. Close the dialog box by clicking OK.

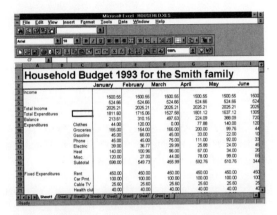

Using borders to divide and outline a worksheet

You can create additional borders to delineate ranges and categories; it's up to you. Your goal should be to make the worksheet easy to read.

Using borders in charts

You can also use borders in charts. There are no rows and columns to separate, but you may wish to outline text fields to make your charts neater and more attractive.

Outlining supplemental chart text is easy; try it on the text field we added to the Household Budget chart (see Chapter 6). Switch to the chart window by double-clicking the chart. Select the text field and choose **Cells...** from the **Format** menu. Click the "Patterns" tab.

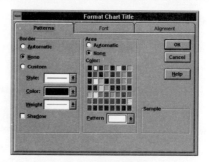

Adding borders to charts

Click the "Automatic" option button (followed by OK) to place a border in a predetermined weight, style and color around the text element. Click "None" to remove the border.

Now you can select the desired style, color and weight for the border. Each of these options has a list box for showing the selections available. Click the down arrow to the right of the option field to open the list box. When you select an entry from the list, it appears in the option field and the list box closes. Try it.

If you also check the "Shadow" check box at the lower-left, so it contains an X, a shadow is added to the border.

As you make your selections, you can see how the border will look by checking the sample in the box on the lower right. When you are satisfied with the effect, close the dialog box by clicking OK.

Adding color to text, cells and borders

Before you get too creative remember, unless you have a color printer, colors are good for screen display only. If you only have a black and white printer, you can still use them. The printer will just ignore the colors so your document will print normally.

Excel offers a palette of 16 different colors. Depending on your computer, you may have many more colors available, but Excel can only display 16 of them. While it is possible to change any of Excel's standard colors by choosing **Options...** from the **Tools** menu and clicking the "Color" tab, the shades provided are more than adequate for clear and attractive documents.

Coloring Fonts

You can color fonts using the **Cells...** command from the **Format** menu, clicking the "Font" tab. Let's make our Household Budget workbook title dark blue. Select cell A1 and select **Format/Cells...**.

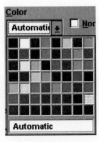

In the center is a "Color" field that is normally set to "Automatic". This means Excel assigns a predetermined color (the default is black). Click the down arrow to the right of the field to open the "Color" list box.

Set the font color

A set of color "swatches" appears. Click the dark blue color button. The color will appear in the "Color" box, and the list box will close. Close the dialog box by clicking OK.

Select any other cell contents and color them if you wish. Use **Cells...** from the **Format** menu each time. You can also do this for chart text.

Coloring cells

You can also apply a background color to one or more cells. Let's see how a soft yellow would look for the row of total income:

1. Select the appropriate cells for the subtotal for Fixed Expenditures.

2. Choose **Cells...** from the **Format** menu and click the "Patterns" tab.

3. Open the "Pattern" list box by clicking its down arrow.

4. Select the fine hatching pattern.

5. Click the yellow color button.

6. Watch the "Sample" field for the result of combining this foreground color with the hatching pattern.

7. Close the dialog box by clicking OK.

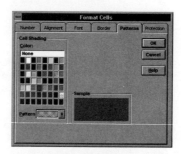

Setting cell color

The selected cells now appear in pale yellow. Repeat the process for the other total lines. The top line could be given a darker yellow. It's all up to you. You can apply colored areas to chart elements using the same principles. This is discussed in Chapter 6. Text fields, chart backgrounds and entire chart surfaces can also be colored this way.

Coloring borders

To create colored borders, just select **Cells...** from the **Format** menu and click the "Border" tab. Select the desired color from the "Color" list box. The sample border will change to the selected color. After completing your other border selections, close the dialog box by clicking OK.

Borders on charts are created differently, as we discussed earlier. However, the dialog boxes should all work the same way.

Automatic Formatting in Excel

If you lack the time, desire or artistic inclination to dress up your worksheets in the many ways we just described, the **AutoFormat...** function is for you. This function leaves formatting to Excel.

First select any cell within the worksheet to be formatted, except the first or last cell (A1 and O28 in our example). Excel will figure out where the table begins and ends. The second row and column (cell B2) is a good choice. Then choose **AutoFormat...** from the **Format** menu.

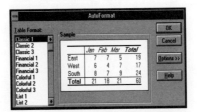

The AutoFormat function

The dialog box includes a list of available formats. When you select one, a sample appears for previewing. Click OK if that's the one you want, and the entire worksheet is formatted accordingly. If you don't like the results, immediately choose **Undo AutoFormat** from the **Edit** menu.

AutoFormat variations

You can also apply autoformatting to your worksheet, then make minor changes manually, using the techniques you just learned.

Problems Polishing Your Work

None of the techniques discussed in this chapter can really ruin your worksheet. And you really can't lose any data. At worst, you might not like the worksheet's appearance, but then it's very simple to undo the formatting if you haven't made further revisions. The **Edit** menu always gives you an **Undo...** command for the preceding action.

I want to use a font that isn't listed

Your selection of fonts depends on what fonts have been installed on your computer. You'll probably have at least five or six fonts available. You have to add that font to your system in order to use it.

Using too many different fonts can detract from clean-looking documents. We chose Arial for our example because it is generally available and looks good in print as well as on screen. Be careful not to make your document gaudy.

A whole column has disappeared

There are two reasons why you might get this annoying problem. Either you have manually reduced the column width to 0, or you have accidentally selected **Format/Column/Hide**. In either case, you can easily correct the problem:

1. Determine which column is missing by checking the column coordinates for the missing letter.

2. Select the columns on either side of the missing one by dragging across the adjacent column coordinates.

3. Choose **Format/Column/Unhide**.

4. The missing column reappears.

A row of text is cut off at the top and now I can't read it

This happens when a row height setting is too small for the font you're using. The problem is easily corrected. Select any cell in the affected row, and choose **RowAutofit** from the **Format** menu.

My cell and range borders don't look right

This is not surprising, considering the confusing way Excel handles borders. The best solution is to remove the affected borders and start over. Select the affected cell or range, choose **Cells...** from the **Format** menu, and click the "Border" tab. Click the five border position fields as many times as necessary to clear them. Then click OK to close the dialog box.

To remove all borders from the entire worksheet, first select the worksheet by clicking the upper-left corner (where the row and column coordinates intersect). Then remove the borders as described above.

After coloring cells, I can't read their contents anymore

Most likely, you've chosen the same color for both font and background. Select the problem cells and choose **Cells...** from the **Format** menu. Click the "Pattern" tab. Open the "Pattern" list box by clicking its down arrow. Select the "None" option (the top entry in the list), then click OK.

If you don't have the font color set to white, the cell contents should now be visible. If you do, select the cells again and choose **Cells...** from the **Format** menu. Click the "Font" tab. Open the "Color" list box by clicking its arrow. Find the entry "Automatic" (at the bottom of the list) and click it. Then click OK and the cells should now contain black text on a white background.

Chapter 8

Printing With Excel

In most cases, once you have put the finishing touches on your worksheet, you will probably want to print it. Besides having a printer connected to your computer, you must have the Windows interface set up to use the printer. Normally printer setup is done when Windows is installed (see Chapter 3). If you install a printer after installing Windows, you do the setup at the time of the installation.

In the last section of this chapter, we briefly explain how to set up a printer for use under Windows. You can either do this yourself or ask someone who is familiar with Windows to help you.

Your printer may limit how creative you can be in designing your worksheet, because it may not be able to produce all the creative touches Excel offers you. A worksheet's appearance also depends on whether the appropriate setup procedures have been performed.

Selecting the Right Printer

If more than one printer is connected to your system, or if you use a different computer to print your worksheet, be sure to select the printer that will actually be used for printing. Make sure you do this early in your worksheet development, before any special formatting takes place.

Choose the **Print...** command from the **File** menu. This dialog box includes several options that we will discuss later in the chapter. For now, click the Printer Setup button.

Printing With Excel

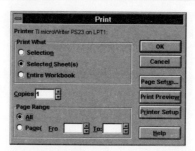

Click the [Printer Setup] button in this dialog box

The following dialog box appears:

Select the printer you want to use

Your computer may only show a single entry in the printer list. If it shows more than one, click the name of the printer you plan to use.

QUICK TIP

If you're familiar with your printer, click [Setup...] in this dialog box. A new dialog box appears; its format varies depending on the printer you selected. Here you can choose settings for your printer's features. Of course, if the setup has already been done, even outside of Excel, this isn't necessary. Click [OK] to close the "Printer Setup" dialog box, and you'll return to the "Print" dialog box.

If the printer you want now is different from the one you chose when you set up your worksheet, Excel may display a warning that the worksheet's appearance will change. If you really want to change printers, just click [OK] to acknowledge the message. Be sure, however, to preview the changes and reformat your worksheet where necessary for the new printer.

Changing the Output's Appearance

The various options in the "Page Setup" dialog box control the exact appearance of your output on the printed page. Choose **Page Setup...** from the **File** menu to get this dialog box.

You can also choose the **Print Preview** command from the **File** menu at any time. This displays the pages of your worksheet exactly as they will print. The print preview screen contains a [Setup...] button. Clicking this is another way to get to the "Page Setup" dialog box.

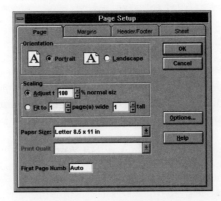

Dialog box settings for the Household Budget worksheet

The first "Page Setup" option determines the orientation of the printed page. Pages can be printed in portrait (11" long and 8 1/2" wide) or landscape (8 1/2" long and 11" wide) orientation. Usually the worksheet is wider than it is high, so landscape orientation is probably best.

The "Paper Size" list box, opened by clicking its down arrow, will show all the paper sizes defined for the selected printer. Choose the size of paper you wish to use.

Be sure to load the printer with paper that's the requested size.

CAUTION!

8 | Printing With Excel

You'll probably print on 8 1/2 x 11 inch paper most of the time, especially if you are using one of the popular laser printers.

In the "Margins" tab, indicate how much space you want between the text area and the edges of the page. These settings can also be changed later. Common margin values are 0.75 for left and right, and 1.0 for bottom and top.

For now you can ignore the remaining options. Close the dialog box by clicking (OK).

Determining What to Print

You probably won't print an entire worksheet very often, so Excel lets you determine just what gets printed. Even if you want to print the entire document, it is best to request it explicitly. This is called setting the print area:

1. Select all the cells of your worksheet that are to be printed. In our example, this is the range from A1 through O66 (including the defined charts).

2. Choose the **Print...** command from the **File** menu.

3. In the "Print What" group, choose the "Selection" option button and click (OK).

Page breaks

After setting the print area to include only selected cells, you may notice that dotted lines appear on your worksheet. These lines indicate page breaks.

In other words, where each of these lines appears, a new page will begin when you print the document. It is common for a worksheet to occupy several pages.

Excel determines page breaks automatically, using the paper size and margin settings you select. If you do not explicitly select an area, Excel will print all cells containing data.

Previewing What Will Print

When you choose **Print Preview** from the **File** menu, the worksheet is displayed on the screen exactly as it will appear when printed. Here you can see the results of the settings you have just made, including printer, page orientation, paper size and margins. Of course, you'll only see the portion included in the print area.

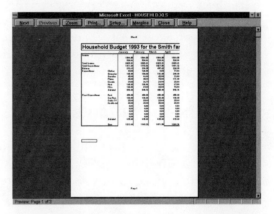

Seeing how the printed output will look

The bar at the bottom of the screen shows how many pages there are, as well as which page is currently displayed (for example, "Preview: Page 2 of 2"). At the top of the screen are several buttons.

Next and Previous are used to go to the previous or next page. Zoom gives an enlarged view, about equal to an actual printout, and provides scroll bars so you can move around in zoom mode.

To leave zoom mode and return to reduced size, click the page or the Zoom button again.

The mouse pointer looks like a magnifying glass in **Print Preview**. When you click anywhere on the page, you automatically zoom in on that area.

Print...	Produces a dialog box that allows you to initiate printing.
Setup...	Gives you the "Page Setup" dialog box, where you can change any of the settings discussed earlier.
Margins	Toggles the display of margin and column borders on/off.
Close	Returns you to the worksheet window.

It's always a good idea to preview your documents before printing. You can make sure that page breaks are where you want them and that fonts are what you expect. Any changes needed to polish your documents can then be made before wasting paper on unfinished printouts.

Improving Worksheet Printouts

Print Preview gives you additional ways to improve the appearance of documents directly before printing. A simple one involves the manipulation of margins. You can see the results of these manipulations as you're making them.

Setting margins

If you can't see the dotted margin lines, first click Margins to display them. You can then reposition the margins by dragging their handles. As you move a margin, its current setting is updated on the status bar below the display. When you release the mouse button, you confirm your new settings and the rows and columns are automatically redrawn.

This method of adjusting margins makes it easy to place the data correctly on the printed page. If you need a little more room to fit everything in, try making the margins narrower.

> At the top of the page are handles for column borders. Drag these handles to adjust the column width on the printed page as well as the worksheet. Of course, this adjustment affects the screen display when you return to the worksheet window.

QUICK TIP

Page margin settings made in **Print Preview** apply to all the pages you print. Unfortunately, you cannot vary them from page to page within a worksheet.

Centering page contents

Other fine-tuning is performed in the "Page Setup" dialog box, which you can call by clicking the [Setup...] button. The "Center on Page" group (click the "Margins" tab) has two check boxes, "Horizontally" and "Vertically", for centering data automatically. If you check either of these, you divide the available margin space so they're the same height, width or both. This works especially well with one-page workbooks.

Automatic page scaling

The "Scaling" option (click the "Page" tab) is a handy feature. By clicking "Fit to", you can determine how many pages the worksheet will occupy. Type the number of pages that should make up the printout's width and height.

If you type "1" for both dimensions, the entire worksheet (or the printable area) is scaled to fit on a single page. Unfortunately, this can also distort the data or make the font so small that it's illegible.

Used with care, however, it can be very useful. In our example, suitable dimensions might be 2 pages wide by 1 tall. This makes an excellent printout.

Special settings

Click the "Sheet" tab. If you click the "Row & Column Headings" check box so an X appears there, the coordinates (A-IV and 1-16384) will print along the left and top borders of the worksheet.

Printing With Excel

If the "Gridlines" check box is enabled, the gridlines between cells (otherwise visible on the screen only) are also printed. Presumably you would use this option only if you have not placed your own borders around worksheet cells.

The "Black & White" option is useful if you display your worksheet with colored fonts, cells or borders, but print it in black-and-white. Without this option, various hatching patterns replace the colors and can make your worksheet look cluttered and unattractive. When the option is checked, all fonts and borders are printed in black and all cell backgrounds in white, giving the worksheet a cleaner appearance.

Adding headers and footers

Every page of your document can have a header and a footer. The basic content of headers and footers is the same for all pages. Excel automatically determines their placement, regardless of your margin settings.

In the Print Preview window, if you notice that part of your worksheet is hidden by headers or footers, you have to adjust the margins accordingly.

The dialog box for adding headers and footers is called by clicking the "Header/Footer" tab in "Page Setup".

If you want to add custom headers or footers, click the [Custom Header...] or [Custom Footer...] button. Within each dialog box, you define the contents of the header or footer in three separate sections (left, center and right). As you type text into one of the three edit boxes, it automatically wraps to the next line when you reach the right border. To go to a new line manually, type [Alt] + [Enter].

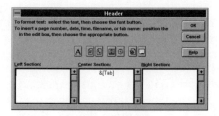

Creating a header

In addition to normal text, you can insert placeholders for certain information. For example, to create a header showing the current page and the total number of pages in the left header section, you would proceed as follows:

1. Click the edit box entitled "Left Section".

2. Type "Page" followed by a space.

3. Click the button containing the number in the center of the dialog box. The control code "&P" appears after your typed text. It serves as a placeholder for the current page number. When the first page is printed, the header will contain the number 1 in place of the control code, the next page will contain the number 2, and so on.

4. Behind the control code, type a space, "of" and another space.

5. Click the button containing the two plus signs. The control code "&N" is inserted. At print time, this is replaced by the total number of pages.

Let's say you also want the center section of your header to show the document name. Click the center edit box. Type "Worksheet" followed by a space. Now click the button containing the Excel icon. The control code "&F" is inserted. Later, the worksheet file name will replace it.

Finally, in the right header section you could put the time and date, using the calendar and clock buttons to insert the appropriate control codes.

Close the dialog box by clicking [OK]. When you return to the Print Preview window from the "Page Setup" dialog box, you can zoom in on the header to verify its contents.

Starting to print

You can initiate printing directly from the Print Preview window using the [Print...] button. From the normal worksheet window, choose **Print...** from the **File** menu. Either method produces the same dialog box.

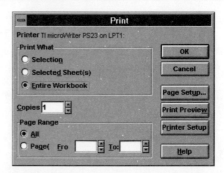

Selecting what to print and starting to print

The "Entire Workbook" option causes all pages to be printed. If you want to print only part of your document, enter the appropriate page numbers in "From" and "To". You can also set the desired number of copies now. The remaining options can be ignored. Click [OK] to start printing.

Possible Problems Printing With Excel

Next we will discuss a few troubleshooting tips, in case things go wrong in printing your worksheet. Here are some of the most common problems and their solutions.

No printer to select

You chose **Print...** from the **File** menu. In the dialog box that appeared, you clicked the [Printer Setup] button. The next dialog box, the "Printer" list box, showed no printer selections. This can happen if your printer is not correctly installed for use in Windows. So now you have to install a printer.

You could call in an expert. However, all you really need to do is follow the simple instructions on the next page to do it yourself.

Before you begin, restart Windows, know the name of your printer, and gather the original Windows diskettes and any diskettes that came with the printer.

1. Open the "Main" program group.

2. Double-click the "Control Panel" icon.

3. Double-click the "Printers" icon. The "Printers" dialog box appears.

4. Click the [Add >>] button. The dialog box is expanded to include a list of printers at the bottom.

5. Select your printer from the list and click [Install...]. If your printer is not shown, select the top entry ("Install Unlisted or Updated Printer") and click [Install...].

6. Place the original Windows diskette or one that was supplied with the printer into the drive, and click [OK].

7. In the subsequent dialog box, select the name of your printer and click [OK]. The printer name will then appear at the top of the "Installed Printers" list in the "Printers" dialog box.

8. The printer port is given as LPT1: (displayed as "... on LPT1:"). This is your computer's first parallel port. In most cases this will be correct. If you know that it isn't, you can assign a different port. To do this, click the [Connect...] button and select the appropriate port from the choices shown.

9. The [Setup...] button opens a dialog box that allows you to make selections for your printer's configuration. The options available depend on the type of printer; they usually include paper source, paper size and orientation. Some printers have options for color printing or special printer fonts.

After configuring your printer, try a sample printout to see if everything works as expected. If you still have problems, you may have to consult a friend or dealer.

Fonts look bad when printed

You are no doubt using fonts that are only suitable for screen display. Select the parts of your worksheet that are affected and change to a TrueType font (indicated by a double T). These look good both on screen and in print.

Cell contents do not print

If your cells have a colored background and you have a black-and-white printer, the background may be printed in black, obliterating the text inside the cell. The best way to solve this is to choose **Page Setup...** from the **File** menu, click the "Sheet" tab, then click the "Black & White" check box. All cells will now print as white with black text.

Worksheet covers the headers and footers

You have defined a header and/or footer for your worksheet, but the worksheet covers it. Excel places headers and footers in fixed positions on the page. If your worksheet margins are too narrow to allow for them, the worksheet data will overlap them.

The easiest way to correct this problem is to move the margins in "Preview" mode. If the dotted margin lines are not visible, click the Margins button to display them. Then drag the margin handles until enough room is available for the headers and footers.

Chapter 9

Excel As A Database

Excel can easily do simple data management. This chapter explains this aspect of Excel, using a collection of addresses as the example. You will see how easy it is to automate your old index cards or address book by creating a database to hold your addresses.

Records and Fields

Obviously, your index card system or address book is useless if it isn't organized. Each address contains a name, address and phone number, and all the entries are arranged the same way. For instance, your friend or relative's name comes before the address.

In our database, each address occupies one card. The following figure illustrates our database's structure:

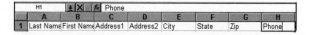

A conventional database for address management

We arranged the address information so the last name is first, a standard way to look up someone's name. After this, we list the rest of the address in a standard arrangement, with each piece of information in its own place.

At some point, you'll delete some addresses and add others, to keep your information up to date. It's easier to do this in a computerized "address book".

9 | Excel As A Database

Records

To make a database in Excel, you start by setting up an ordinary worksheet. Each address occupies one row, called a record.

Fields

The information for each friend or relative is arranged the same way. Each piece of information occupies its own column, called a field. Our worksheet requires column headings for all the fields, so our address database will be structured in tabular form. Each column will be a field, and each row a record.

Creating a Database

Before creating the address database, close all open worksheet windows by double-clicking each one's control box (the square containing the minus sign in the upper-left corner). The control box is on the far right side of the menu bar in windows enlarged to their full size. If Excel warns that you have to save changes to the worksheet, click [Yes]. Then the window will close.

After you close the last window, the Excel menu bar displays only two menu names. Choose **New...** from the **File** menu. Click "Worksheet" in the dialog box that opens, if it isn't selected, then click [OK] to close the dialog box.

You now have a clean worksheet window. If the window is not full size, click the triangle pointing up at the right end of the title bar to maximize it.

Entering field names

First you need to enter names for the data fields in the top row of the worksheet. Select cell A1. Type:

```
Last name
```

Press the ⏎ key to confirm your entry and move the pointer to the next cell, B1. Do this again for the next field name, using the field names in the illustration on page 151 as a guide.

Make the field names boldface so readers can see them clearly. Select the appropriate cells (A1 through I1) and click the bold toolbar button (the "B").

When you finish the headings, save the worksheet. Choose **Save** from the **File** menu. You can save it in the directory that's currently open, or in another one. Then enter the name of your file in the text box, "File Name":

```
Address
```

Click OK, and Excel saves the worksheet.

Defining the database range

Excel still doesn't know this worksheet will be used as a database. Select a range of the cells with the field names and the following row of empty cells (A1 through I2). Choose **Set Form...** from the **Data** menu. When Excel prompts you whether it should assume that the header row is the top row of the selection, click OK.

Entering records

When you choose **Form...** from the **Data** menu, the following appears:

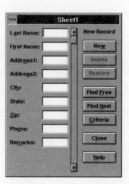

The data form controls access to the database

CAUTION!

> You can't access the data form until you define a database range. Make sure you define it correctly, or the data form won't be any use.

On the left side of the form are a number of edit boxes, which match the fields in our address database. This is where you enter all your information. The cursor appears in the top edit box, "Name", so enter the first surname here. Then move to the next edit box by clicking it with the mouse or pressing [Tab].

WARNING!

> Be careful not to press [Enter] when you complete each entry. If you do, you won't have a chance to fill in the other fields.

The text may not appear to fit, because you may not see everything in the data form. But the database will display the entire contents. When you're done filling in all the edit boxes, click [New]. Did you notice that the data is in the second row of the worksheet? Excel automatically extends the database range.

The data form remains on screen and the edit boxes are cleared so you can continue to enter information. For our example, enter four rows of information. When you're finished, close the data form by clicking [Close]. Now you can see the address records on the worksheet.

To make any changes or corrections, select the appropriate cell and click the formula bar. Enter your change or correction, then click the green checkmark or press [Enter]. You can also use the data form to change records. **Choose Form...** from the **Data** menu.

The data form with records

This time, the data form shows the data for the first record. Above the New button, the current record and the total number of records are shown (in the example, 1 of 4).

You can glance through the records. Click Find Next and the contents of the second record appear in the input fields. Excel automatically updates the current record number.

Click Find Prev to glance at a previous record. Excel beeps at you if you are already in the first record when you do this. The same thing happens if you click Find Next when you are at the last record. Don't worry that you might be messing up the database or information because you're not.

When the form displays the record you want to change, click the appropriate edit box and make the correction. The change is applied to the database as soon as you do something else, like page forward or backward, or close the data form.

If you need to page through a lot of records in a large database, use the scroll bar next to the edit boxes. Click the up or down arrow to move to the previous or next record, respectively. If you click the bar below the scroll box, the last record (always blank) appears. Click the bar above the scroll box to move to the first record. You can also drag the scroll box to move to any position in the database range.

As we mentioned, the last record is always blank. When you want to add a new record to the database, do one of two things:

- Scroll down to this record. Then fill in the blank input fields with the appropriate data and click New.

- Click New to clear the input fields. The data you enter is saved as a new record when you click any command button. You don't have to click New again.

To delete a record, use the data form to locate it then click Delete. Click Yes to confirm the command. Cancel the command if you issued it by mistake or change your mind.

Adding new fields

Adding a new field is as simple as adding a column to a worksheet. Select the column to the left of the place where you want the new column, by clicking the column coordinate at the top of the worksheet. Then choose **Column** from the **Insert** menu and a new empty column is inserted. Enter a name for the new field in the first row of the new column.

Adding a column as a new data field to the right of the existing fields is done the same way. Reset the database range. Select the entire database again, including the new column, and choose **Form...** from the **Data** menu.

QUICK TIP

When you open the data form again (by choosing **Form...** from the **Data** menu), you see the new field. Initially, every record is blank. You can enter information for each record now.

Formatting the address database workbook

It's helpful to know some basic workbook formatting. For example, use the "Autofit" option for the columns comprising the database. Select the columns, then choose **Column/AutoFit** from the **Format** menu.

To dress it up a little more, try one of the autoformatting styles. Select the database (including the blank row at the bottom), choose **AutoFormat...** from the **Format** menu, and select "List 2" for the database.

Sorting

Before sorting, you have to select what will be sorted. Excel sorts by rows or columns. You usually select rows in a database, because they contain the data records. Exclude the top row of field names and the bottom row of blanks. In our example, select A2 through I5, then choose **Sort...** from the **Data** menu. The "Sort" dialog box appears:

The Sort dialog box determines the range to be sorted

Select "Last Name", located under "Sort By" in the upper-left portion of the dialog box. It may already be selected.

Now specify whether you want the last names to be sorted alphabetically from A to Z ("ascending" order), or from Z to A ("descending" order). Numbers precede the letters in "ascending" order, and come after the letter in "descending" order.

Click OK when you have finished specifying how you want Excel to sort the rows. If your database contains a lot of records (say, more than 1,000), sorting could take some time. You can also re-sort, using different specifications.

Searching for records

Use the data form to search for a particular record in a database. Choose **Form...** from the **Data** menu. Excel opens the "Form" dialog box.

Click the Criteria button to clear the edit boxes so you can enter your criteria. Enter the data you want to find. If you want the record for Mr. Smith, for example, click the "Last Name:" edit box and type:

```
Smith
```

Fill in any other fields you need to, then click Find Next. The form displays the record you want or, if nothing matches your criteria, it displays the first record. If several records meet your search criteria, use Find Next and Find Prev to view them one at a time.

If you aren't sure exactly how to type what you're looking for, use a question mark in place of one or more letters or numbers. Maybe you can't recall how to spell Mr. Smith's name. Was it Smithe or Smythe? Type "Sm?" in the "Last Name:" edit box to find all the records of people with these two letters beginning their last names:

```
Sm?
```

You'll see records for the Smalleys, the Smeads, as well as Mr. Smith. To stop searching and return to viewing all records, click "Criteria" again. Click "Clear" to clear the search fields.

Problems Using Excel As A Database

You can make only one big mistake when you use your worksheet as a database. If you don't set the database range correctly, nothing will work properly. You won't even be able to display the data form.

If you make this mistake, select all the database cells, from the top row of field names to the blank row along the bottom. Choose **Form...** from the **Data** menu. Then all the database management techniques will be available.

Chapter 10

Features To Simplify Your Work

We've described many, but not all, of Excel's features. You have enough information to use Excel from Chapters 3 through 9. This chapter offers some additional features that customize and simplify your work.

Custom Number Formats

Chapters 4 and 7 discussed using number formats to specify how numbers, including dates and times, appear in cells. Open the "Number Format" dialog box by choosing the **Cells...** command in the **Format** menu and clicking the "Number" tab. Do this in your Household Budget worksheet now.

The Format Cells dialog box

This displays a list of categories on the left side and the selected category's format codes in the center. Select the "Number" category. Its format codes are as follows:

10 | Features To Simplify Your Work

Format	Shows
0	The number as an integer. A fractional number is rounded to a whole number.
0.00	The number with two decimal places. A number with more than two decimal places is rounded. Excel adds one or two trailing zeros to a number with fewer than two decimal places.
#,#00 and #,##0.00	The number with commas separating the thousands. Unlike the zero placeholder, the pound sign placeholder is used to keep places open for numbers other than zero before the decimal point.
#,##0_);(#,##0) or #,##0.00);(#,##	The negative number in parentheses.

The last two formats let you show the negative numbers not only in parentheses, but also in a different color. You can choose from black, blue, cyan, green, magenta, red, white, and yellow.

Define a custom number format at any time, simply by selecting a category and format code from the "Number" dialog box. Your format code selection appears in the edit box, where you can make changes. Practice this in your Household Budget worksheet with this example:

1. Select cell D3 and then choose **Cells...** from the **Format** menu.

2. Click the "Number" tab, and click "Number" in the "Category" list box.

3. Click the format code "#,##0.00_);(Red)(#,##0)".

4. Click the "Code" edit box and change the format code to "[Blue]#,##0.##;[Red]-#,##0.##", then click OK.

You can use your custom number format now. When you open the "Format Cells" dialog box again, it will be included in the list. Here you can also choose to display numbers with currency symbols (like $), percentage signs, fractions (using the backslash) and scientific notation. Delete it if you don't want it there.

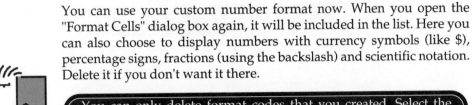

You can only delete format codes that you created. Select the custom format code, then click Del.

CAUTION!

Customizing the date and time

When you customize date and time entries in the "Date" category for your workbook, use spaces, periods, backslashes (/), hyphens or colons to separate the day, month and year. Letters represent the units of time; choose from one of the following options:

Letter	Option
d	Day number, no leading zero in single-digit days (1-31)
dd	Day number, including leading zero (01-31)
ddd	Weekday abbreviated to three letters (Sun-Sat)
dddd	Weekday not abbreviated (Sunday-Saturday)
m	Month abbreviated without a leading zero (1-12)
mm	Month abbreviated with leading zero (01-12)
mmm	Month name abbreviated to three letters (Jan-Dec)
mmmm	Month name not abbreviated (January-December)
yy	Year abbreviated to two digits, with leading zero (00-99)
yyyy	Year not abbreviated (1900-1999)
h	Hour without leading zero (0-23)
hh	Hour with leading zero (00-23)

Features To Simplify Your Work

Letter	Option
m	Minute without leading zero (0-59)
mm	Minute with leading zero (00-59)
s	Second without leading zero (0-59)
ss	Second with leading zero (00-59)
AM/PM or am/pm	Time with this notation
A/P or a/p	Time with this notation

QUICK TIP

Excel's internal clock displays midnight as 0:00:00 and the moment before that as 23:59:59. This is important when entering times.

Using Styles

You should always format similar workbooks by using similar features such as font, size, border and alignment. For printing, Excel lets you group these format selections and assign them a single format called a style. After you define the style, you can select it for any cell or range, from the style list box.

Choose **Style...** from the **Format** menu to display the "Style" dialog box. Experiment with this on your Household Budget worksheet. Create a dark blue heading on a light yellow background:

1. Select cell A1. This contains the workbook title with the various features you assigned to it in Chapter 7.

2. Select **Style...** from the **Format** menu.

3. Clear the current entry, then type:

    ```
    Title
    ```

4. Press Enter to confirm your entry.

Your new style will appear in the style list box as "Title". Try using it now:

1. Select cell A3.

2. Select **Style...** from the **Format** menu.

3. Select "Title" from the list of styles. Click (OK).

Cell A3 is now formatted the same as cell A1. Whenever you want to define a new style, just select an example of that style from the worksheet, type a new name in the style list box, and press (Enter).

When you click the (Modify...) button, the dialog box expands, as you can see in the following figure:

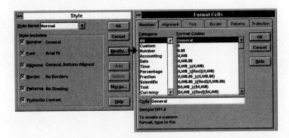

The Format Cells dialog box

Delete a style you don't want anymore by clicking (Delete). Choose formatting features with the check boxes in the "Style Includes" group. The corresponding page lets you access the dialog boxes you need to edit the options in the "Style Includes" group. Change settings in the dialog box and click (OK).

Then click (OK) again in the "Style" dialog box to confirm the style change. This change is immediately reflected in your worksheet. When you open the "Style" dialog box again, your changes will be reflected in the description of that style.

Features To Simplify Your Work

The Spellchecker

Excel's Spellchecker ensures that worksheet text is all spelled correctly. The Spellchecker checks each word against its built-in dictionary and lets you know if it doesn't recognize a word. If your word is correctly spelled, ignore this warning. If it is misspelled, correct it manually or choose from a list of suggested spellings.

Excel automatically checks the spelling of all the text below and to the right of the selected cell. If you only want to check the spelling of a portion of the worksheet, select a range. To check the entire worksheet, select cell A1. Choose **Spelling...** from the **Tools** menu to open the "Spelling" dialog box:

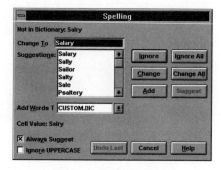

The Spelling dialog box

When the Spellchecker stops at an unknown word, it displays the following at the top of the dialog box:

Not in Dictionary: (unknown word)

It displays a suggested spelling under "Suggestions", and displays the closest match at the top of the list and in the "Change To" edit box. Decide whether to:

- Keep your word the way it is. Click Ignore to skip over this word or Ignore All to skip over all occurrences of this word. You could also Add this word to a custom dictionary for later reference. The spellchecker uses your custom dictionary along with its built-in dictionary.

- Accept the suggested spelling shown in the edit box. Click Change to accept it in place of this word or Change All to accept it in place of every occurrence of this word.

- Choose another suggested spelling from the list. Select your choice and click Change or Change All.

- Change the spelling manually. Type this in the "Change To" edit box and click Change or Change All.

The program continues checking the worksheet or range after you finish with this word. When it completes its check, it lets you know. If you want to stop checking spelling before the program is done, click Cancel. Always save your worksheet after you have checked spellings, to save these corrections.

The Spellchecker tells you when it is finished

Using Macros

When you create a worksheet, you often need to perform the same steps repeatedly. Excel lets you "program" this series of steps so you can access the sequence later just by pressing a key combination. This is called a macro. To create a macro, do the following:

1. Determine all the actions (menu commands, mouse operations, etc.) that make up this series of steps.

2. Practice the steps and make notes to be sure the sequence is complete.

3. Choose **Record Macro/Record New Macro...** from the **Tools** menu, which opens the "Record New Macro" dialog box:

Creating a macro

4. Name the macro. It can be almost any length, but can't include any spaces. For this example, use Excel's default name, "Macro1".

5. Click [Options>>]. Click "Shortcut Key:" in the "Assign to" group. Type a letter in the edit box, next to "Ctrl+". When you access the macro in the future, you use this key combination.

6. Confirm the option button "This Workbook" is enabled, then click [OK] to close the dialog box.

Now Excel begins recording, and displays the word, "Recording", on the lower-left part of the screen. Perform the actions you want to record. Be careful not to make any unnecessary steps, and to "click" as little as possible. After you finish, choose **Record Macro/Stop Recording** from the **Tools** menu to let Excel know you're done. All the recorded actions will be stored as a macro under the name you assigned.

Would you like to replay the actions you recorded in the macro? All you need to do is run it, by entering the key combination that accesses it. You can also run a macro this way:

1. Choose **Macro...** from the **Tools** menu.

2. Select the macro you want to run from the list of names in the dialog box.

3. Close the dialog box by clicking `Run`.

Now the macro will run. Feel free to record and save more macros, but keep in mind that you are limited to less than 26 macros, due to the limited number of letters. Also, Excel already uses some of these letters for its menu commands If you choose to assign macros to menus instead, you are limited to 15 macros.

Chapter 11

What Not To Do In Excel

If you understand the previous chapters, you know how to operate Excel and produce high-quality worksheets. It's just as important to know how to avoid problems in Excel. You should observe the following precautions whenever you use your computer and the Windows interface.

Don't switch off your computer while Excel is running

QUICK TIP

When you save your worksheet, don't assume that all the data is properly stored right away. You also have to exit Excel. If you switch off the computer without exiting the application, you may not be able to open your worksheet when you start Excel again.

> Always remove any diskettes in the disk drives before you switch off the computer.

Never switch off the computer until you exit Excel and Windows, regardless of whether you have data to save. Make sure the drive lights are off as well. All that your computer should display is the familiar prompt:

C:\>

Don't switch off your computer while Windows is running

Switching off the computer while Windows is running can have unpleasant consequences. Use the following steps to properly terminate a work session:

What Not To Do In Excel

1. Store your worksheet, using the **Save** command from the **File** menu.

2. Close Excel by selecting **Exit** from the **File** menu. You return to the Windows Program Manager.

3. Close Windows by choosing **Exit Windows** from the Program Manager's **File** menu.

4. Click OK in the dialog box that follows.

The Program Manager saves certain settings on the hard drive that it needs to properly start Windows the next time. It's okay to switch off the computer now, because the screen only displays the prompt:

C:\>

Don't work directly off diskettes

Whether you're in Excel or another application, never work strictly off diskettes. The computer requires more processing time when it has to access information from diskettes. Excel won't even function unless it is loaded onto your hard drive. Any worksheets you want to use should be copied onto your hard drive as well. Place them in an Excel directory.

Don't remove a diskette while the disk drive is operating

Say you load a worksheet from the diskette to the hard drive so you can work with it. When the worksheet is complete, you copy it back to the diskette. Before you remove the diskette from the disk drive, be sure to glance at the drive light first and make sure it isn't blinking.

Don't install or remove cables while the computer is running

Your computer has cables connecting the keyboard and monitor to the central processing unit, the mouse to the keyboard, the central processing unit to the wall outlet, etc. Depending on which cable you tamper with, you can cause serious damage. Make it a rule never to install or remove cables until you have exited any applications and programs that are running, then switched off the computer.

Don't rename the directory containing Excel

You can rename files and directories in Windows, but be careful not to rename the directory that contains Excel. This is usually called C:\EXCEL. If you change the name, you will have to make extensive changes to the Excel program icon before you could restart Excel.

QUICK TIP

> Do not change this or any other directory names that were automatically created when you installed Excel.

Chapter 12

Overview Of Important Functions

Use this chapter as a reference whenever you use an Excel function in your worksheet. When you choose **Function...** from the **Insert** menu, a dialog box opens, with a list of functions. You can find an explanation for the function you select from this dialog box.

AVERAGE(Range reference or list)

This function returns the average value of a range or list of values. For example:

```
=AVERAGE(1,2,3)
```

or

```
=AVERAGE(A1:C1)
```

gives

```
2
```

In the above example, the reference to A1:C1 refers to cells A1, B1, and C1 containing the values 1, 2, and 3, respectively.

COUNT(Range reference)

This function returns the number of filled cells within a range. In the Household Budget worksheet, for example, a cell with the formula

```
=COUNT(B1:Q35)
```

gives

```
430
```

This means the range of cell B1 through cell Q35 has 430 filled cells.

=IF(Condition,then,else)

This function lets you make one cell's contents conditional on the value in another cell. For instance, suppose you want cell A5 to contain the word, "Yes", if another cell has a value of 1; otherwise, cell A5 should contain the word, "No". This conditional cell would contain the formula:

```
=IF(A40=1,"Yes","No")
```

If you enter the value 1 in cell A40, the word "Yes" appears in cell A5. If you enter any other value in A40, "No" appears.

INT(Number)

This function returns an integer for a decimal number that was entered into the formula. It deletes the decimal point and the following numbers from the decimal number. Say you put the following formula in a cell:

```
=INT(987.6876876)
```

The cell's value is 987. This function doesn't round the decimal number to the nearest integer.

MAX(Range reference or list)

This function returns the highest value from a range or list of values. For instance:

```
=MAX(1,2,3)
```

gives

```
3
```

MIN(Range reference or list)

This function returns the lowest value from a range or list of values. For example:

```
=MIN(1,2,3)
```

gives

```
1
```

NOW()

This function returns the current date and/or time. You have to select the cell and determine the date/time format. Say you choose the format h:mm. The function

```
=NOW()
```

might return

```
11:39
```

RAND()

This function returns a random value between 0 and 1.

ROUND(Number,Number of places)

This function returns a rounded value for a decimal number entered in the formula. This number is rounded up or down, depending on whether it was closer to the greater or smaller value. In the function, you also have to specify the number of fractional places. The formula

```
=ROUND(9987.675439,3)
```

gives

```
9987.675
```

12 Overview Of Important Functions

SQRT(Number)

This function returns the square root of a number.

SUM(Range reference or list)

This function returns the sum of a range and/or list of values. Use any combination of single cell references, ranges and constants. But remember to separate references with semicolons. For example

```
=SUM(D3:S3,A40,R99)
```

gives the sum of the range of cell D3 through S3, plus the value in cell A40, plus the value in cell R99.

TODAY()

This function returns the current date. Select the cell and determine the date format. To illustrate, use the format m/d/yy. The following formula

```
=TODAY()
```

may give

```
8/5/93
```

Refer to Chapter 13 to find out more about functions.

Ready-To-Use Formulas

You can use Excel functions to devise your own formulas. This chapter discusses a few formulas that you can use for a wide variety of purposes. Instructions follow each formula, and include formatting and other tips. They should give you some ideas for your own formulas.

Calculating with Dates and Times

Performing calculations with dates is one of Excel's handiest features. If you have a database containing birth dates, for example, Excel can calculate each person's age automatically (We discussed databases in Chapter 9).

Enter the number format m/d/yy in two cells. Then enter the current date, using the TODAY() function, in the first cell. In the second cell, enter the person's birth date. Enter the formula to calculate the difference between the current date and the birth date in a third cell. For example,

```
=B2-C2
```

Add the value 1 to the current date, so Excel can recognize the birth date when it falls on the current date. This changes the formula to read:

```
=(B2+1)-C2
```

Assign the number format yy to the third cell. The person's age, in years, will appear here. If you want to be more precise, especially for infant ages, show the result in months. Use the number format mm.

Ready-To-Use Formulas

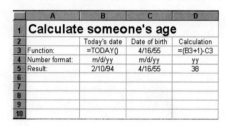

	A	B	C	D
1	**Calculate someone's age**			
2		Today's date	Date of birth	Calculation
3	Function:	=TODAY()	4/16/55	=(B3+1)-C3
4	Number format:	m/d/yy	m/d/yy	yy
5	Result:	2/10/94	4/16/55	38
6				
7				
8				
9				
10				

Calculating a person's age

You can also perform calculations with time values. The NOW() function returns the current time. Remember to assign a number format to the cell to display the result properly.

You can also determine the weekday on which a given date falls. Choose a date from the future or past. Use the WEEKDAY() function.

Enter the number format m/d/yy in the first cell, then enter the date you want to check. Enter the number format dddd in the second cell, then enter the WEEKDAY function and the first cell reference. For example, enter this formula:

```
=WEEKDAY(B6)
```

Excel calculates the weekday on which this date falls, and displays it in the second cell.

	A	B	C	D
1	**Calculate day of week**			
2		Date to check	Weekday	
3	Function:	2/10/94	=Weekday(B15)	
4	Number format:	m/d/yy	dddd	
5	Result:	2/10/94	Thursday	

Determining the weekday for a given date

Gambling with Excel

Can you think of a practical application for the random number function RAND()? See if the following example generates any ideas.

This example simulates rolling a die. The results must be values between 1 and 6. Write the formula as:

```
=INT(RAND()*((6-1+0.5)+0.5)+1)
```

This formula includes the integer function INT, to make sure the results are whole numbers. Substitute a different integer value for the value 6 if you want to change the range of results.

TAKE NOTE

> Excel returns the first result as soon as you confirm the formula you typed with Enter. For each subsequent "roll of the die", press F9 to recalculate the worksheet formulas and produce a new result.

	E	F	G
1		**Die-rolling simulation**	
2			
3		Function:	=INT(RAND()*((6-1+0.5)+0.5)+1)
4		Number format:	0
5		Result:	6
6		Note:	Press <F9> to roll again.

Generating random integers from 1 to 6

Calculating Payments, Taxes, and Other Fun Figures

Excel contains many financial functions. We use two in this section to spark your imagination.

Say you plan to take out a loan. You know the loan amount, annual interest rate, and term. From this, you can calculate the monthly payment. The following figure illustrates this calculation:

	A	B	C	D	E
1	Calculate monthly loan payments				
2		Annual %	Term (months)	Principal	Payment
3	Example:	0.0975	36	$25,000.00	=ABS(PMT(B5/12,C5,D5))
4	Number format:	10%	0	$#,##0.00	$#,##0.00
5	Calculation:	12%	36	$750.00	$24.91

Calculating the installment on a loan

Use the data in the above figure to experiment with the PMT() function. The PMT function calculates the installment payments on a loan over a specified period.

Conversely, you can use the PV function to determine the amount you can borrow, given a monthly payment, interest rate, and term. The following figure illustrates this:

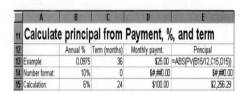

	A	B	C	D	E
11	Calculate principal from Payment, %, and term				
12		Annual %	Term (months)	Monthly paymt.	Principal
13	Example:	0.0975	36	$25.00	=ABS(PV(B15/12,C15,D15))
14	Number format:	10%	0	$#,##0.00	$#,##0.00
15	Calculation:	6%	24	$100.00	$2,256.29

Calculating the amount you can borrow

Use the percent sign (%) in your formula to calculate percentages. For instance, enter the following formula in a cell:

```
=(45.67*30%)
```

This returns the value 13.701, which is 30% of 45.67.

Sometimes you also need to calculate the total amount as well as the percentage, for instance, in calculating sales tax. The following figure shows how to calculate the tax and figure the total amount.

	A	B	C	D	E
21	Calculate total price (with MI sales tax)				
22		Amount	Sales tax	Calculate sales tax	Total
23	Example:	$998.67	4%	=B25*C25	=B25+D25
24	Number format:	$#,##0.00	0%	$#,##0.00	$#,##0.00
25	Calculation:	$102.00	4%	$4.08	$106.08

Adding sales tax to a net total

It's more complicated to figure this out when you have a total amount and want to know how much tax is included and what the item amount is. The following figure shows the best way to calculate this:

	A	B	C	D	E
31	Calculate price				
32		Total	Sales tax	Calculate sales tax	Item price
33	Example:	$998.67	4%	=B35-E35	=B35/(100+(C35*100))*100
34	Number format:	$#,##0.00	0%	$#,##0.00	$#,##0.00
35	Calculation:	$106.08	4%	$4.08	$102.00

Calculating tax from a total

Determining Quantity Discounts

Some of Excel's functions go beyond simple calculating. Logical functions, for example, let you enter a value in a cell that is dependent on conditions met in other cells. The IF() function, in its general form, looks like this:

```
IF(Condition,then,else)
```

The condition is a normal logical comparison, such as: if 1 is greater than 0, the result is TRUE(); if 2 is greater than 0, the result is FALSE(). The condition's true value is checked within the IF() function and, if the result is TRUE(), the "then" value is placed in the cell containing this formula. If it is FALSE(), the "else" value is placed in the cell.

Say you want to compute invoice totals. Given a minimum quantity, a special discount is applied. The discount rate and minimum order size that qualifies for the discount are the constants. In the cell where the invoice total will appear, enter the following formula:

```
=IF(E3>D3,(B3*E3)*(1-C3),B3*E3)
```

Ready-To-Use Formulas

This formula assumes these cells contain the following entries:

```
B3 = Unit price
C3 = Rate of discount
D3 = Minimum order quantity
E3 = Actual order quantity
```

The following figure illustrates this:

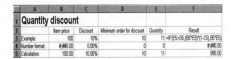

	A	B	C	D	E	F
1	Quantity discount					
2		Item price	Discount	Minimum order for discount	Quantity	Result
3	Example:	100	10%	10	11	=IF(E5>D5,(B5*E5)*(1-C5),B5*E5)
4	Number format:	#,##0.00	0.00%	0	0	#,##0.00
5	Calculation:	100.00	10.00%	10	11	990.00

Calculating a quantity discount

The IF() function lets you perform calculations that depend on given conditions in other cells. Such flexibility offers almost unlimited possibilities.

Chapter 14

Excel Terms You Should Know

This chapter lists important Excel terms. Use it as a reference when you come across an unfamiliar term or want to understand a workbook concept.

Application window

See **Excel window**.

ASCII

Acronym for "American Standard Code for Information Interchange". An ASCII file contains pure text, with no formatting (e.g., bold, alignment codes). You can open this sort of file in almost any program or application, including Excel.

Boot

This is another term for starting your computer. It refers to everything that happens in the computer system from the time you switch on the computer until it displays the DOS prompt or the Windows screen. Rebooting the computer is also called warm starting the computer.

Cell

The smallest unit of a workbook. A cell can be empty or can contain text, numbers, or a formula. A column and a row intersect at a cell, and this is how the cell is referenced. For example, where column A (the first column) and row 1 intersect, you have cell A1.

DOS

Acronym for "Disk Operating System". Your computer's operating system is a system of programs that allow the computer to understand you. Yours might be called MS-DOS, DR DOS, or something similar. Without the operating system, the computer and you cannot communicate. The operating system controls the mouse, keyboard, monitor, disk drive, hard drive, etc.

Element

The individual parts of a chart. There are text elements (chart title, axis labels, etc.), graphic elements (axes, bars, columns, etc.), and the chart surface. When you change any chart element properties (size, color, position, etc.), follow the basic rule of Excel: First select, then operate.

Excel window

Also known as the application window; the first window to open when you start Excel. From this window, you can open one or more workbook windows. The Excel window contains the usual window elements, most importantly Excel's operating controls: The menu bar, toolbar and formula bar.

Formula

A set of instructions for performing calculations on the contents of a cell or range. A formula always begins with an equal sign (=), followed by numbers (constants), references (variables), operating symbols (+, -, *, / and ^), and/or functions. A simple formula would be one that adds the values of two cells: =A1+B1. The sum appears in the cell containing this formula.

Function

A self-contained operation the Excel program provides to help simplify your work. Each function consists of a name and a pair of brackets enclosing any numbers or references that the function will evaluate. Access functions by choosing **Function...** from the **Insert** menu. Select the function you need from the dialog box that opens. Excel then inserts that function in the formula bar.

A simple function would be SUM(), which you use to add the contents of cells and/or ranges. =SUM(A1:Q35) adds the values of all the cells in the range of cell A1 through cell Q35.

Print area

The area of the workbook that you want to print. If you want to print only part of a workbook, define the part to be printed. Select it, then choose **Set Print Area** from the **Options** menu. You can redefine the print area at any time.

Range

A selection of adjacent cells. A range's reference is made up of the range's upper-left cell reference and lower-right cell reference, separated by a colon. For example, A1:Q35 designates the range of cell A1 through cell Q35.

Range name

The name for a range, used in formulas to represent the range. After you select a range, choose **Define Name...** from the **Formula** menu. Type a range name, up to 256 characters long and consisting only of letters and numbers, and the underline character as separator. You can't use spaces in the name.

Reference

The way a cell or range is specified. Each cell has a reference composed of a column coordinate (A-Z and AA-IV) and a row coordinate (1-16384). A range has a reference consisting of the upper-left cell and lower-right cell references, separated by a colon.

Spreadsheet

Another term for workbook.

Table

A range of cells suiting a specific purpose. A workbook can contain more than one table.

14 | Excel Terms You Should Know

VGA

Acronym for "Video Graphics Array". The video graphics array controls your computer screen's display. It makes sure the information to be displayed is sent to the screen and displayed correctly. The VGA is one graphics array standard; another is the Super VGA, or SVGA.

Windows

Windows is a graphical user interface, which means that it simplifies your operation of an application. When Windows is running, you see windows and icons on the screen and can manipulate them using the mouse. You need Windows to run Excel.

Workbook

A grid made up of columns and rows, also known as an electronic spreadsheet. You can include tables and charts in a workbook. You can also use a workbook as a database. The blank workbook offers 256 columns and 16,384 rows but, when you save your workbook, Excel deletes any unused columns and rows. Excel saves workbooks in files.

Workbook window

The visible part of the workbook. When you start Excel, the application window is open and the workbook window is part of it. The workbook's title bar, at the top of the window, shows the workbook name. Excel's default name for a new workbook is "Book" followed by a sequential number.

The workbook window displays only part of the workbook. For the most working space, maximize the workbook window. The workbook will take up the entire Excel window, and its name will be displayed in the Excel window's title bar.

Excel Sheets

The ready-to-use workbook included with this book will help you use Excel more efficiently. In this workbook, you'll find sheets that can be used for professional or personal use. You can quickly and easily select the correct sheet and then adapt it to your needs.

The examples are designed to clearly demonstrate all Excel's capabilities. You'll find that the better you are at using Excel, the more you will gain from the examples.

However, we cannot guarantee that the examples will produce the correct solutions in all cases. So, for important applications, perform a rough calculation yourself to check Excel's results.

Excel 5.0 Standard

All the sheets in this workbook require Excel Version 5.0 or higher and can be used with Windows-based computers. For information on how to expand the workbook, refer to Chapter 4.

Some of the sheets can be sorted. To sort, select the cells, then click one of the "Sort..." toolbar buttons ("Sort Ascending" or "Sort Descending"). Or, select the cells and select **Sort...**, from the Data menu, select the sort criteria, and then click OK.

Avoiding copying and pasting rows directly above or below a heading. If you do this, the pasted row may not be formatted correctly.

A | Excel Sheets

Installation

Installing the workbook is quite simple. All the data on the diskette come in packed format; they have been compressed into an archive file. In order to use the workbook and its sheets, this file must be copied to the hard drive and then unpacked. This is handled by the Abacus SETUP application included on the companion diskette for this book.

First start Windows and insert the 3.5-inch diskette into the corresponding drive (either A or B). Then, from the **File** menu, select the **Run...** command. In the "Command Line:" text box that appears, enter:

A:SETUP

If you're using Drive B:, enter:

B:SETUP

Then confirm the entry by clicking (OK).

The SETUP application now starts. When you click the (Continue) button, the archive file is copied onto the hard drive and then unpacked. By doing this, the installation program automatically creates a file, on Drive C:, called XL_BEG.

Using the Workbook

You can start the workbook in Excel with the command **File/Open...**. Select the file named COMPDISK.XLS. Click a sheet tab to select a sheet.

The headings and formulas in each sheet of the workbook can be changed according to your own preferences if data-protection is switched off.

However, you should be very careful when changing formulas. The formulas are compact and can be defined to refer to other cells in the sheet, either absolutely or relatively. So, it's difficult to read them. The advantage of this method is that you can create and edit sheets very quickly. Change a formula only if you are sure, and only if you understand how it works.

Remember, you can easily create your own sheets by using the example sheets. Open the workbook, make the desired changes as necessary and then save it as a new workbook.

Column width, line height, font

Because of the graphics or text display used by your computer, all texts and numbers may not be readable. If this happens, switch off data-protection and change the column width or line height until you can see both numbers and text clearly.

Data-protection, cell-protection, file-protection

For formulas and other input data, Excel offers the option of protecting data on a cell-by-cell basis. This feature is called cell-protection. All cells, except for input cells, in the sheets described in this appendix start with protected cells.

Cell-protection works in a given sheet only when file-protection is also switched on. All the sheets in this book have file-protection on by default to prevent accidental deletions. You can switch off this file-protection with the Excel command **Tools/Protection/Unprotect Sheet...**.

This command must be entered, for example, prior to changing cells that are not input cells or enlarging column width or line height. The same also applies when changing type or window-locking. To switch on file-protection again, use the Excel command **Tools/Protection/Protect Sheet...**.

For a detailed description of cell- and file-protection, refer to the Excel user's manual.

Input values

Input values generally appear in blue type and/or within a blue margin. Also, most input values are displayed in italics, so you can identify them on black-and-white monitors.

A | Excel Sheets

Results

Results are usually indicated by green type and green margins. Instructions, headings, and other sheet texts generally appear in black.

Window-locking

Some sheets have labels fixed at the upper-left corner. This means that when you use the scroll bar, these fields do not move. You can cancel window-locking by first switching off data-protection and then selecting the Excel command **Window/Unfreeze Panes**. To activate window-locking again, select the Excel command **Window/Freeze Panes**.

For more information on window-locking, refer to the Excel user's manual.

Copying and pasting

Some sheets are set up so you can expand them almost indefinitely by simply copying rows. Always check the tips to see if this applies to your particular sheet.

When data-protection is switched off, it's possible to expand the sheet as desired. You can do this, for example, by copying a row with blank input fields (within the shaded area) and then simply pasting it directly in front of the row. To paste more than one row, repeat the procedure.

When copying and pasting, always use the Excel commands **Edit/Copy**, immediately followed by **Edit/Paste**. This ensures that the row you've copied will be pasted in front of the selected row properly. This means that its entire contents (not just the blank input fields but also the formula-derived computations) are copied.

For a detailed description of this command sequence, refer to the Excel user's manual. It's also possible to paste several rows simultaneously. However, until you are an experienced Excel user, use the above step-by-step method.

Printing

Sheets can be printed in any size. To check a sheet's appearance, use the Excel command **File/Print Preview**. After you've selected **Print Preview**, you can also change the appearance by clicking on the [Setup] button. Another way to change the layout is by entering the Excel command **File/Page Setup...**.

The sheets are set up to conform to standard letter size (8 1/2 x 11 inches). If you want to use a different format, cancel this automatic adjustment by using the **File/Page Setup...** command. When the dialog box appears, click the "Page" tab, and select the "Adjust to ... normal size" option button in the "Scaling" group. Then type the desired scaling, or click on the up/down arrows. Many of the examples, such as the address and telephone directory, should be printed in a smaller size.

If you have a color printer, such as the HP Deskjet 550C or 500C, you can also print the sheets in color.

For additional information, refer to your Excel user's manual.

Changing the print area

If you want to print more than what's selected, you can change the print area. For more information, refer to the Excel user's manual.

Templates

Many sheets can also be used as blank templates. To generate a blank template, do the following:

Click the sheet tab you want and select the cells which can accept input (the blue cells, in most cases). Select **Edit/Clear/Contents** then save the template using **File/Save As...**.

A | Excel Sheets

Miscellaneous Sheets

In this section, we'll present some sheets that have various uses. For example, you'll find sheets for calculating dates and times, and converting typographical units of measurement. Each sheet is listed by general type and sheet tab name.

Date/Time Calc

This sheet converts the difference between two date inputs into years, months, weeks, days, hours, minutes, and seconds. Time of day can also be included in the calculation.

Section of Date/time calculation sheet

Time-of-day Calculation

This sheet converts the difference between two time-of-day inputs into hours, minutes, and seconds.

Typographical Conversion

This sheet converts measurements between mm, inches, pica, points, and Didot points. In this conversion sheet, enter the desired number into the "Input Value" column. The result of the conversion immediately appears in the same row, in the desired units.

Copy Enlarger|Reducer

This sheet helps you determine what degree of enlargement or reduction you need to make photocopies of different sizes. For example, if your copy is 10 inches wide and you want it to be 8 inches wide, you would enter 10 in the "Current length" column, then 8 next to it in the "Length you want" column. The "Set machine to" column tells you the percentage to put into the copying machine.

Automobile Sheets

The sheets in this section can be used for information about automobiles. There are templates and sheets for auto expenses, fuel consumption, braking distance, braking times, and lease calculations.

Auto Expenses

This sheet provides a way to organize automobile expenses. Enter the vehicle number at the upper-right in the blue input field. The sheet lists totals as well as individual values, and also includes a calculation for fuel consumption.

Gas Mileage

This sheet lets you calculate your gas expenses and mileage. In order for the fuel consumption figure to be accurate, you must fill up the gas tank each time, and enter both the odometer reading and the gallons purchased in the appropriate columns.

Braking Dist. | Time

This sheet determines an automobile's braking distance, braking time, reaction distance, stopping distance, and stopping time.

A | Excel Sheets

The following input values must be given: Braking Delay, Reaction Time, and Speed. Typical values are: Braking Delay of 10 m/sec^2 with a reaction time of 1 sec. A car's maximum braking delay is often listed in the technical section of the owner's manual.

Remember that these values apply only under ideal road conditions. Poor weather (rain, snow, ice), bad roads (loose pavement, uneven surfaces), and poor vehicle maintenance (tires, brakes) can significantly lower the actual deceleration.

Reaction time can also be significantly impaired due to physical factors (alcohol, drugs) as well as psychological ones (distractions, stress). Such factors will automatically increase the stopping distance, especially at high speeds.

Auto Comparison

This sheet compares the prices of automobiles with various features, including the base sticker price. It computes monthly expenses based on usage values plus additional costs (to be entered accordingly).

Leasing 1

Calculates the cost of a lease based on regular fixed monthly payments. For comparison purposes, you can also use the same calculations for a loan (payments to be made on the first day of each month).

The final result includes interest amount, total amount paid, monthly payment amount, and a comparison of leasing and credit, with accumulated interest and approximate effective annual interest.

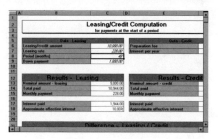

Section of Leasing 1 sheet

Leasing 2

This sheet calculates the costs of a lease based on regular fixed monthly payments. The result consists of costs incurred when the lease is terminated, based on the actual remaining balance with and without sales tax.

Section of Leasing 2 sheet

Speed Conversion

This sheet converts speed measurement from miles per hour to feet per second, and vice versa.

Financial Sheets

Of all the uses of Excel sheets, the ones designed for finances are probably the most interesting but also the most complicated. In this section you will find sheets for expenditure control at different periods, credit card expenditures, recurrent payments, loan calculations, and a vacation budget summary.

Expense List

This sheet keeps track of receipts, expenditures, and other payments.

Expenses-Daily

Use this sheet to keep track of daily expenditures.

Expenses-Weekly

This sheet keeps track of weekly expenditures.

Expenses-Monthly

Use this sheet to keep track of monthly expenditures.

Expenses-Yearly

This sheet keeps track of annual expenditures.

Check Register

CHECKS.XLS

Use this sheet to organize check expenditures.

Credit Cards

Use this sheet to keep track of credit card expenditures.

Section of Credit Cards sheet

Ongoing Expenses

Use this sheet to keep track of all recurrent payments.

Capital Comp

This sheet calculates the final value of a capital investment on the basis of regular fixed monthly payments and a constant rate of interest. You can adjust for payments made either at the beginning or the end of the month.

Results include the number of payments, interest, amounts paid, and interest credited.

Payoffs (Loans)

This sheet calculates monthly loan payments on the basis of regular fixed monthly payments and a constant rate of interest. It also differentiates between payments made at the beginning of the month and at the end of the month.

Results include the number of payments, interest, amounts paid, and monthly payment amount.

Mortgage Scenarios

This sheet calculates the monthly payment amount for a number of loans on the basis of regular fixed monthly payments and a constant rate of interest for each loan. Each payment is credited on the first day of the month.

Results include the number of payments, interest, amounts paid, monthly payment amount, and the total of all payments/accumulated value.

A | Excel Sheets

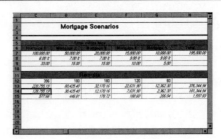

Section of Mortgage Scenarios sheet

Vacation Expenses

Use this sheet to determine vacation expenses.

Business Sheets

Excel sheets can be used for various business applications. For example, you can use them for supply summaries and invoices to product comparisons and market value analyses.

Goods Sold

This sheet keeps track of goods sold (inventory). A value for order probability can also be entered. This sheet calculates total valuation, with and without order probability, average weighted order probability, and number of items. You can also enter anticipated turnover for the current quarter and later.

Daily Ledger

Use this sheet as a daily journal for receipts and expenditures, including value-added tax. It provides totals for deposits, value-added tax, and disbursements, and it calculates the balance.

Account Journal

Use this sheet to check bank statements with deposits and withdrawals (without value-added tax). This sheet gives totals for deposits and withdrawals, along with the balance.

Quarterly Sales

This sheet keeps track of goods sold (order inventory). You can obtain a liquidity forecast by entering the following formula into the respective cells of the quarter columns:

Invoice

This sheet provides varying rates of value-added tax and gives the net amount, value-added tax, and total amount.

Expand this sheet according to your own preferences, if you wish. Refer to Chapter 4 for further information.

Collection Sheets

Excel sheets can also help you manage various types of collections. In this section you'll find sheets that can be used to organize books, slides, CDs, cassettes, videotapes, and photographs.

Book Filecard

This is an index file sheet for keeping track of a collection of books. The books are listed according to the date they were purchased.

This sheet can also be used as a blank form.

Slideshow Card

This is an index file sheet for keeping track of slides. The slides are arranged according to the date they were taken.

A | Excel Sheets

You can expand this sheet to accommodate almost any number of slides or number of exposures per film. For expansion according to the number of exposures within a slide film, see Chapter 4.

For expansion according to the number of slides, instead of a single row, copy an entire block and then paste the block directly in front of the copied block. Refer to Chapter 4.

This sheet can also be used as a blank form.

CD Collection

This is an index file sheet to keep track of CDs, which are arranged according to the date they were purchased. You can expand the sheet to accommodate almost any number of CDs or number of selections per CD.

For expansion according to the number of selections within a CD, see Chapter 4. For expansion according to the number of CDs, instead of a single row, copy an entire block and then paste the block before the copied block.

This sheet can also be used as a blank form.

Cassette Library

Index file to keep track of music cassettes. The music is arranged according to its position on the tape (counter).

You can expand the sheet to accommodate almost any number of tapes or number of selections per tape. For expansion according to the number of selections within a tape, refer to Chapter 4. For expansion according to the number of tapes, instead of a single row, copy an entire block and then paste the block before the copied block.

This sheet can also be used as a blank form.

Video Library

This is an index file for keeping track of self-produced videotapes. The tapes are arranged according to their position on the tape (counter).

You can expand the sheet to accommodate almost any number of tapes or number of selections per tape. For expansion according to the number of selections within a tape, see Chapter 4. For expansion according to the number of tapes, instead of a single row, copy an entire block and then paste the block before the copied block.

This sheet can also be used as a blank form.

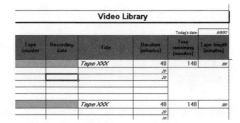

Section of Video Library sheet

Photos

Use this sheet to keep track of dates photographs were taken. By changing the headings, this sheet can be adapted to a variety of other uses.

You can also reduce the summary by percentages to any time-management format.

This sheet can also be used as a blank form.

Household Sheets

You can use these sheets for tasks around the house, such as measuring tiles and calculating living space.

A | Excel Sheets

Tile Computation

This sheet takes entries for area measurements, tile size, etc. and calculates the amounts and prices of tiles, joint sealant, and tile adhesive. The formulas are based on a square surface, with no tiles being cut. Since this almost never happens, you should expect some non-square areas and tile cutting, by allowing for a few extra tiles.

Living Space

This sheet takes entries for area measurements, numbers of rooms, etc. and calculates the total living space. You can also adjust for plaster deduction.

Organization Sheets

Use the sheets in this section to organize various information.

Phone Messages

This sheet can be used as a checklist to keep track of telephone calls.

You can adapt this sheet for various uses by changing the headings (with data-protection switched off). It's also possible to reduce the summary by percentages to any time-management format.

This sheet can also be used as a blank form.

Project Checklist

Use this sheet as a checklist for keeping track of activities or a project in progress. In the "Effect" column, you can enter such things as savings, costs, personal effects, yields, and expenditures. The total of all these columns is listed in the adjacent "Running total" column.

You can adapt this sheet for various uses by changing the headings. Reduce the summary by percentages to any time-management format. This sheet can also be used as a blank form.

Daily Planner

This sheet is a daily planner. This summary has a weekly format and can be started on any date. However, you should start the week on a Monday.

To personalize the sheet, switch off data-protection. The schedule can be adapted to a variety of uses by changing the headings. It's also possible to reduce the summary by percentages to any time-management format. For more information, refer to Chapter 4.

This sheet can also be used as a blank form.

Weekly Planner

This sheet is a weekly planner. This summary has a weekly format and can begin on any date. However, you should start the week on a Monday.

To personalize the sheet, switch off data-protection. The schedule can be adapted to a variety of uses by changing the headings. You can reduce the summary by percentages to any time-management format.

This sheet can also be used as a blank form.

Monthly Planner

This sheet is a monthly planner divided into days and double periods. This summary has a monthly format and can begin on the first day of any month.

To personalize the sheet, switch off data-protection. The schedule can be adapted to a variety of uses by changing the headings. You can reduce the summary by percentages to any time-management format.

This sheet can also be used as a blank form.

A | Excel Sheets

Personal Information Sheets

You can also use Excel sheets for personal information, such as keeping track of your current weight, and creating birthday lists, address lists, telephone directories, etc.

Weight Control

Use this sheet to keep track of the weight of five people. This sheet can also be used as a blank form.

Loan Card

You can use this sheet to keep track of items you've loaned to others. This sheet can also be used as a blank form.

Birthday List

Use this sheet to keep track of birthdays. This sheet can also be sorted and used as a blank form.

Address File

Use this sheet to organize addresses. This sheet can also be sorted and used as a blank form.

Phone Book

Use this sheet to organize telephone and fax numbers. This sheet can also be sorted and used as a blank form.

Blood Alcohol

This sheet can be used to estimate blood alcohol level after drinking. The table on the right lists typical quantities of various drinks and their alcohol content. To estimate blood alcohol, enter the drinks with quantity and alcohol content in the left table and then specify the number of drinks you've had.

It's also possible to change the number, quantity, and alcohol content of the drinks, and add new types of drinks.

Catering

Use this sheet to calculate the costs of throwing a party. You can enter the number of people invited and their names. You can also enter the number, price, and type of drinks as well as the average meal cost per person.

The sheet provides the total cost of the party and the average cost per person.

Section of Catering sheet

Recipe Conversions

Use this sheet to convert quantities of recipe ingredients, based on the number of people served. From the original number of people, you can obtain quantities for two alternative counts.

This sheet can also be used as a blank form.

Conversion Sheets

Conversions of all types can be very useful. With the following sheets, you can easily calculate lengths, weights, areas, and dry measures, along with temperature and power units.

A | Excel Sheets

Metric Lengths

MET_LIN.XLS

This sheet converts the U.S. system of measurement to metric lengths.

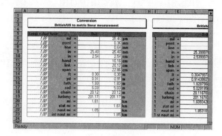

Section of Metric Lengths sheet

US Linear Measurement

US_LIN.XLS

This sheet converts from one to another American length. Enter the desired number into the "Input Value" column. The result of the conversion immediately appears in the same row, in the desired units.

Metric Lengths

This is a unit and conversion sheet for metric lengths. Enter the desired number into the "Input Value" column. The result of the conversion immediately appears in the same row, in the desired units.

US-Metric Measurement

This sheet converts American units of area measurement to metric units of area measurement.

Metric Areas

This sheet converts metric areas. Enter the desired number into the "Enter value here" column. The result of the conversion immediately appears in the same row, in the desired units.

Metric Cubic Units

This sheet converts American units of volume measurement to metric units of measurement.

Metric Volumes

This is a conversion sheet for American dry measures to metric dry measures.

Metric Weights

This is a conversion sheet for American weights to metric weights.

Weight Conversion (Metric)

This is a unit and conversion sheet for metric weights. Enter the desired number into the "Enter value here" column. The result of the conversion immediately appears in the same row, in the desired units.

Temperature Conversion

This is a conversion sheet between degrees Celsius, Kelvin, Fahrenheit, Reaumur, and Rank. Enter the desired number into the "Input Value" column. The result of the conversion immediately appears in the same row, in the desired units.

A | Excel Sheets

Energy Conversion

This is a conversion sheet between joules, int. joules, meter-kilograms, kilocalories, and hp-hours. Enter the desired number into the "Input Value" column. The result of the conversion immediately appears in the same row, in the desired units.

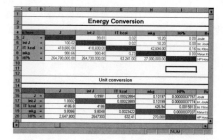

Section of Energy Conversion sheet

Travel-Related Sheet

The sheet in this section can be used for determining currency conversions.

Currency Conversion

This sheet converts exchange rates. Enter the unit rate of exchange and the sheet converts dollars to foreign currency and foreign currency to dollars.

This sheet can also be used as a blank form.

Sports Sheet

Sheets are especially suited for sports statistics. They provide an easy way to maintain and evaluate statistics.

Jogging

This sheet summarizes results of races or training runs. It can be adapted to a variety of uses (e.g., walking) by changing the headings.

You can reduce the summary by percentages to any time-management format.

This sheet can also be used as a blank form.

Appendix B

Banania

Introduction

Banania is a computer game. The main character, Bert, is a janitor who must clean up the warehouse after a gorilla throws banana peels on the floor. The object of this game is to help Bert gather as many banana peels as possible in the shortest amount of time, while trying to avoid the monsters that are trying to catch him.

Installation

First, we'll give you some basic information about what you need to do to be able to play Banania. We'll discuss the system requirements, installing the program on your hard drive, linking the game to Windows, and starting and quitting the game.

Requirements

Banania is a program that was specifically developed for Windows 3.x and will run only in Windows. Use the keyboard and the mouse to play the game.

Creating a backup copy

Before installing your new program, make a backup copy of the original diskette. To do this, insert the original diskette into your 3.5-inch disk drive.

B | Banania

Then, depending on which drive label you use for your 3.5-inch disk drive, type either:

```
DISKCOPY A: A:
```

or

```
DISKCOPY B: B:
```

Follow the instructions displayed by the Diskcopy program. (You could also use a different program to make a backup copy.)

When you install the program on your hard drive, use the backup copy. Store the original diskette in a safe place (i.e., in a place protected from heat, dust, magnetic forces, pets, etc.).

Setup application

Start Windows and select **File/Run....** Click on the [Browse...] button. Change to the drive containing your diskette, then double-click SETUP.EXE. In the window that appears, you can specify the settings:

Install from: The disk drive containing the program diskette (generally you won't need to change this setting).

Install on: The hard drive to which you want to copy the files. The program will suggest a subdirectory. To copy the program to a different directory or drive, click on the [Select] button to set a different drive and directory.

Program Group: The program will suggest a group name. To install the program in a different group, choose the appropriate group from Existing Group or enter a new group name in the left box.

If the group name is new, the program creates it for you.

If you're installing the program in a different drive or directory, after you click on the [Select] button, a new window appears.

The selection box displays all the directories of the specified drive. You can change the drive from the "Drive:" drop-down list box.

To install the program in a subdirectory, choose the subdirectory from the directories displayed in the window and click [OK] to confirm your selection. For a new directory, click on the [New...] button.

After you've confirmed the new directory name with [OK], click [Continue] to continue the installation.

If the diskette contains a file with important information that couldn't be included in the manual, this file will be displayed under "Documents", and you can display the file during installation by clicking on the [Read] button. You can also print this file as you read it.

When the installation is complete, you'll be in the Windows Program Manager.

Starting Banania

Start Windows and click the program group in which you installed Banania. Double-click on the Banania icon to start the game.

After the title screen, a brief demonstration of Bert's (the protagonist's) activities appears. To begin the game, click on the button with the double arrow pointing to the right above the playing area, or press [F2]. Now you're ready to play.

The Game

Bert is a janitor who is supposed to clean a warehouse. An escaped gorilla discovered bunches of bananas in the warehouse and is hiding on the 51st floor. On his way up, he ate several bananas and carelessly threw the peels on different floors.

B | Banania

Bert's job is to pick up the banana peels so the people trying to catch the gorilla won't slip on them. He encounters many obstacles along the way, such as closed doors, large crates, and garbage monsters who want to keep the peels for themselves.

The fewer steps it takes you to collect all the banana peels, the higher your score. However, quick reflexes alone aren't enough; you'll also have to do some thinking to reach your goal.

Now we'll explain the rules of the game and tell you how to play. We'll also show you some strategies for playing the game that will help you move Bert through all the floors of the warehouse.

Game rules

The Banania game board consists of several elements. We'll briefly explain these elements now.

The Demo screen

The menu bar is located at the top of the game board. Directly below the menu bar are the counters. They inform you of the current level of the game and the number of points you have. You can also click on a button to choose any level that you have already played.

216

The counter on the left indicates the number of steps Bert has taken. You can easily identify this counter because it has two of Bert's footprints to the left of the numbers.

The counter on the right indicates which floor of the warehouse Bert is on in his hunt for banana peels. You can recognize this counter by the ladder on the left.

In between the two counters you will see a button with a picture of Bert. Whenever Bert comes to a standstill in the game, you can click on this button with the left mouse button to give Bert another chance to pick up all the banana peels on this floor.

Click on the two buttons to the right and left to send Bert to different floors of the warehouse. Clicking the left button sends Bert back a floor. For example, there may be a floor where you managed to pick up all the banana peels, but you believe there's a better (shorter) path for Bert to take. This is crucial for improving your score. Click on the right button to send Bert forward, one floor at a time.

The playing area is located below the counters. This area shows the floor plan of the floor Bert is currently on. You cannot use the mouse in the playing area; you can only use the mouse in the menu bar and the area containing the buttons.

In the playing area you will see Bert, banana peels, garbage monsters, locked doors, crates, and immovable wall blocks. Bert and the banana peels are displayed in yellow.

There are two types of garbage monsters. These types are different colors and have different intelligence levels. In addition, there are various objects which hinder Bert in his search for the banana peels.

Use the arrow keys to move Bert vertically and horizontally in the playing area.

 Only Bert can pick up banana peels. They cannot be moved in the playing area.

The gray squares are wall blocks, which Bert cannot move even if he uses all of his strength. Even the monsters cannot move these wall blocks.

The light blue squares are crates, which can be moved by Bert and the smart monsters. Either one or several squares can be moved simultaneously.

The dark blue squares are heavy crates that both Bert and the smart monsters can move only if the space behind the crate is empty. You can also move the dark blue squares that have light blue squares in front of them.

The gray blocks with door handles and numbers are doors. They are numbered in sequence, beginning with 1. Bert and the monsters cannot move these doors.

There is a key for every door, with a matching number indicating which door it fits. When Bert passes over a square with a key, the door opens.

The green garbage monsters are the stupid ones. They can't move crates and will follow Bert only if they can see him. When they catch Bert, he must start all over again on that floor.

The mauve garbage monsters, like Bert, are able to move the crates. However, they are intelligent enough to follow Bert even when they don't see him. When they catch Bert, he must start over again on that floor.

Now you're familiar with each component of the game and what it does.

The Menus

The menu bar contains all the commands for opening, saving, and exiting. It also contains a **Help** menu. To select the commands, either click the mouse or press [Alt] along with the underlined letter in the command. Now we'll discuss the commands.

The Game menu

The **Game** menu has five commands, **New**, **Open...**, **Save**, **Pause**, and **Exit**.

New

Choose this command to start a new game, which begins on the first floor of the warehouse. You can also press F2 to start a new game.

Open...

Choose this command to load a game you have saved. To prevent others from playing games you have saved, a dialog box appears, prompting you to enter your name and the password you chose when you saved the game. After you type your name and the correct password, you can resume playing the game starting at the floor you last played on.

Save

Any time Bert finishes picking up all the banana peels on a floor, you can save the game. To do this, select the **Save** command. The next time you want to play this game, you will be prompted to type in your name and a password in a dialog box. Each entry can contain only 25 characters. You must enter a name and password only the first time you save a game.

B | Banania

Pause

To stop Bert and the monsters, select the **Pause** command or press F3. For example, you can pause a game when you must determine a strategy for Bert in his hunt for banana peels.

Exit

To exit Banania (even though Bert still hasn't been to all the floors), either click on Exit or press Alt+F4. If you haven't saved your game yet, you'll be prompted to do so.

The **Options** menu contains the **Single-Step, Sound Fx, Run Level...,** **Change Password...,** and **High Scores...** commands.

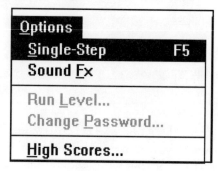

The Options menu

Single-Step

If you don't want Bert to take so long to stop when you press Spacebar, activate Step mode. This allows you to control Bert's every step. Choose Step mode again to return to the previous mode. You can also press F5 to toggle between Step mode and Normal mode.

Sound Fx

This command toggles Banania's sound effects and music on and off.

Run Level...

Select this command to display a list box of all the floors from which Bert has already picked up banana peels. You can choose a floor from this list and send Bert back to improve his score (i.e., reduce the number of steps required to pick up all the banana peels).

Change Password...

Choose this command to change your password. A dialog box appears, prompting you to enter your old password and then the new password. Confirm your new password by clicking on the OK button with the left mouse button or by pressing Enter. In the dialog box, you can either use the mouse or press Tab to switch between the two text boxes and the OK and Cancel buttons.

High Scores...

This command displays the ten highest scores. The high scores are ranked by the following criteria: First, the highest floors are listed. If two scores are saved from the same floor, the score with the lower number of steps is ranked higher. The name of the player also appears. When you save a game, but all ten places on the High Score list are occupied, the lowest high score is removed from the list, if it's worse than the one you're saving.

The **Help** menu contains only one item, **About Banania**. This opens a dialog box containing copyright information and the version number.

Using the Keyboard and Mouse

You must use the keyboard and the mouse to play Banania.

You can operate the menu bar with the keyboard or the mouse. If you use the mouse, simply click on the menu or command to execute the desired action. With the keyboard, press Alt and the underlined letter. This works with menus and commands. You can also use shortcut keys to select functions that are used frequently.

B | Banania

Key(s)	Function
F2	Start new game
F3	Pause key
Alt + F4	Exit Banania
F5	Toggle Step mode on and off

Within the dialog boxes, you can use the mouse to select the desired text box or function. If you prefer to use the keyboard, press Tab to move around in the dialog box and confirm the desired action by pressing Enter or cancel the action by pressing Esc.

You can only use the mouse in the area with the counters and buttons.

When you play the game, you can control Bert only with the arrow keys. Use the arrow keys to move Bert horizontally or vertically or press Spacebar to make him stop. When NumLock is off, you can also use the arrow keys on the numeric keypad.

If you prefer to guide Bert's movements in Step mode, use the arrow keys to control each step he takes.

Game Strategies

While there are no general strategies that apply to each floor of the game, we can give you some pointers that should help you while playing Banania.

Every time you reach a new floor, take a good look at the situation before you start moving Bert. This will give you a good overview of possible dangers posed by garbage monsters or other difficulties.

If you see garbage monsters on a floor, press F3 or choose **Pause** from the **Game** menu to plan Bert's route in advance.

Using Step mode can help or hurt you. When you are in Step mode, remember that Bert will occasionally look around for his navigator. This increases Bert's chances of being caught by a garbage monster that he would outrun if another mode was active. On the other hand, Bert often works too hard, accidentally moving crates that he shouldn't. This blocks his path to the banana peels.

Don't use the keys that open the doors that have monsters behind them. Otherwise, these monsters will chase Bert relentlessly.

Bert can hide from the garbage monsters, since they must see him before they will chase him. Once eye contact is broken off, they won't pursue him as energetically.

Another method of protection from the monsters involves surrounding them with crates and wall blocks. However, remember the smart (mauve) monsters can also move crates. Therefore, they can escape when captured.

The banana peels are also obstacles for the monsters. If several entrances are blocked by banana peels, Bert should open only one of them so that the monsters can't go that far.

Index

PC catalog

Order Toll Free 1-800-451-4319

Books and Software

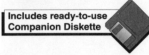

DoubleSpace Without The DoubleTalk

DoubleSpace is the data compression utility included with every copy of DOS 6, and this book is straight talk for anyone who wants to double their hard drive space with knowledge and confidence. This quick guide is the effective way to learn all about DoubleSpace and make the best use of the program. The book discusses what you need to know in short, complete learning units with icons that let the you know in advance just how complicated the unit's topic is. The free companion disk includes several shareware utilities to help ensure smooth DoubleSpace operation.

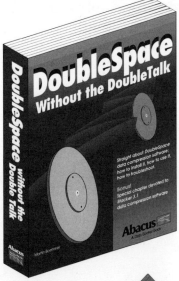

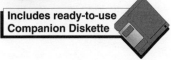

Includes ready-to-use Companion Diskette

The major topics include:
- Hard Drive Compression -What is it?
- Installing DoubleSpace Drives
- Managing and Running DoubleSpace Drives
- Troubleshooting DoubleSpace
- Advanced Techniques
- DoubleSpace Reference

DoubleSpace Without the DoubleTalk walks you through the important preliminary work required for installing DoubleSpace, the concept of data compression, what it does to your drive, and then how to make it really work to your advantage. DoubleSpace can be a dynamic utility with power and features that maxamize your system performance.

Author: Martin Boehmer
Order Item: #B250
ISBN: 1-55755- 250-9
Price: $19.95 US/ $25.95 CAN

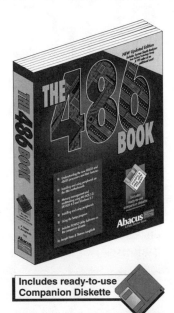

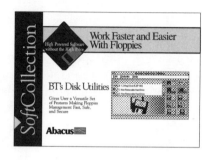

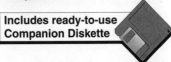

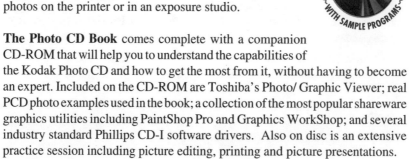

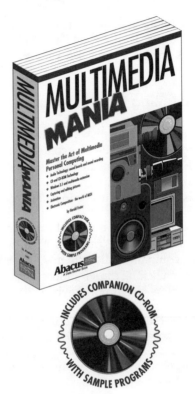

The Companion Diskette

The companion diskette contains two software packages: The exciting Banania Windows game and dozens of great worksheets for Microsoft's Excel.

Installing the Companion diskette

The companion diskette data is compressed. In other words, the files are compressed into smaller files so they will all fit on the diskette. Before you can use the applications on the companion diskette, they must be installed on your hard drive.

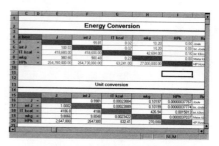

Example of a conversion worksheet from the companion diskette

We've included a special program to make installing the necessary files as easy as possible. When Windows is running, open the Program Manager window and place the companion diskette in your disk drive. Open the **File** menu, either by pointing to it and clicking the left mouse button or by pressing the [Alt] and [F] keys. Select the **Run** menu item (with the keyboard, press [R] or point and click with the mouse).

When the "Run" dialog box appears, type A:\SETUP and press [Enter]. (If your diskette is in drive B:, type B:\SETUP and press [Enter]).

The Abacus Setup program will prompt you for necessary information. You can change the Install From field, if necessary, and change the name of the directory which will contain the executable files from XL_BEG, if you prefer. We recommend that you just accept the suggestions made by Setup and allow the installation process to continue.

The Banania Demo screen

After the Abacus Setup application finishes its task, you'll find a new directory on the hard drive titled XL_BEG.

If the diskette contains a file with important information that couldn't be included in the manual, this file will be displayed under "Documents".

You can display the file during installation by clicking on the [READ] button. You can also print this file as you read it.